Murder and Mystery
In The
PEAK

ROLY SMITH

HALSGROVE

Front cover: *A possible gallows tree?*
On Calton Pastures, near Bakewell

All pictures are by Roly Smith, unless otherwise stated

British Library Cataloguing-in-Publication Data
A CIP record for this title is available from the British Library

ISBN 1 84114 369 3

HALSGROVE

Halsgrove House
Lower Moor Way
Tiverton, Devon EX16 6SS
Tel: 01884 243242
Fax: 01884 243325
email: sales@halsgrove.com
website: www.halsgrove.com

Printed and bound by
The Cromwell Press, Trowbridge

DEDICATION
To Joyce and Charlie Stennett
For half my life, my loving and supportive
Mum and Dad, in loco parentis

Contents

CHAPTER ONE   The Wonders of the Peak   5

CHAPTER TWO   The Old Religion   13

CHAPTER THREE   Arthur and Robin   22

CHAPTER FOUR   Murder and Revenge   32

CHAPTER FIVE   Skulduggery   40

CHAPTER SIX   A Plague on all your Houses   47

CHAPTER SEVEN   Stemples of Doom   56

CHAPTER EIGHT   Ghost Villages   66

CHAPTER NINE   Something in the Air   76

CHAPTER TEN   Modern Murder Mysteries   85

Conclusion   92

Bibliography   94

The allegorical map which illustrated the third edition of Michael Drayton's Poly-Olbion, *showing his Seven Wonders of the Peak* (By courtesy of Prof. Brian Robinson).

4

CHAPTER ONE
The Wonders of the Peak

In one of the earliest descriptions of the Peak, Edward Browne, son of Sir Thomas Browne, writing in his *Journal of a Tour in Derbyshire* published in 1662, found the place a 'strange, mountainous, misty, moorish, rocky, wild country.' An unsurprising description perhaps, considering the author came from the low, cultivated flatlands of Norfolk.

But it is his use of the word 'strange' which is significant. These remote and often misty hills, moors and dales seemed to harbour ancient secrets, myths and legends in a way that the lush meadows and fields of the lowland counties did not. There can be no doubt that it was a strange, mysterious, and even slightly threatening place to these early visitors from the safer, softer underbelly of England.

No one expressed that view better than the cynical traveller, journalist and author of *Robinson Crusoe*, Daniel Defoe, in his *Tour through the Whole Island of Great Britain* published in 1726. 'This, perhaps, is the most desolate, wild and abandoned country in all England,' he said, describing the 'howling wilderness' of the High Peak. And the inhabitants, he thought, were 'a rude, boorish kind of people, but they are a bold, daring, and even desperate kind of fellows in their search into the bowels of the earth...'

Later Defoe was to meet one of these 'desperate fellows' at a lead mine near a place significantly known as the Giant's Tomb on Brassington Moor. As the miner emerged from his shaft, you can almost sense Defoe's impending feeling of horror and loathing as the 'most uncouth spectacle' gradually revealed itself.

For his person, he was lean as a skeleton, pale as a dead corpse, his hair and beard a deep black, his flesh lank, and, as we thought, something of the colour of the lead itself,' wrote Defoe, '...being very tall and very lean he looked, or we that saw him ascend ab inferis, fancied he looked like an inhabitant of the dark regions below, and who was just ascended into the world of light.

Most of those early travellers like Defoe came to the Peak in search of the fabled Seven Wonders of the Peak, a seventeenth-century device designed to reflect the Seven Wonders of the Ancient World to attract visitors. They had been first described by Michael Drayton, the popular Tudor poet who was the son of a Warwickshire butcher, in the third edition of his *Poly-Olbion Or a Chorographicall Description of Tracts, Rivers, Mountaines, Forests, and other Parts of this renowned Isle of Great Britaine* published in 1622. The Seven Wonders soon became an accepted 'Grand Tour' for intrepid travellers from the south, such as Defoe and Celia Fiennes.

As Drayton described them, the 'Wonders' were: the Devil's Arse (Peak Cavern at Castleton); Poole's Hole (Poole's Cavern at Buxton); Eldon Hole (near Peak Forest); Saint Anne's Well (at Buxton); the Ebbing and Flowing well at 'Tydeswell' (Tideswell or Barmoor Clough); 'Sandy Hill' (Mam Tor near Castleton) and the hunting preserve of the Royal Forest of the Peak.

It is significant that many of these 'Wonders' are associated with the Devil or with spirits from the past. Peak Cavern had always been known as 'The Devil's Arse' before Victorian sensibilities sanitised its name, and Peakshole Water which runs out from it was thought by local people to be evidence of the Devil relieving himself. A duck which was dropped down Eldon Hole to find out where it led was said to have emerged several days later through the massive entrance of Peak Cavern – the largest in Britain – having had its feathers singed en route by its apparent passage through the fires of Hell. St Anne's Well at Buxton probably takes its name from Arn or Anu, a Celtic goddess

A Wonder of the Peak – Mam Tor, 'the Mother Mountain'.

after whom the Romans originally named the spa town Aquae Arnemetiae. And Mam Tor, standing proudly at the head of the Hope Valley and ringed by the impressive embankments of a late Bronze Age hillfort, probably has a similar Celtic origin and is thought to mean 'Mother Mountain'.

Drayton's Wonders were later adopted, with the replacement of the medieval Royal Forest by Chatsworth House, by the philosopher Thomas Hobbes in his *De Mirabilibus Pecci: Concerning the Wonders of the Peak in Darby-shire* published in 1636. Small wonder this, as Hobbes was at the time the tutor to the Cavendish children at Chatsworth, and he knew on which side his bread was being buttered.

Charles Cotton of Beresford Hall in Dovedale later translated Hobbes's long-winded Latin hexameters into English, and astutely had his *Wonders of the Peake* (1681) published in the surrounding towns and cities, from where most visitors to the Peak came and still come, to great public acclaim.

Thus the way was opened up for Browne, Defoe and others to explore the strange, mountainous wilderness of the Peak, and report their findings to a fascinated readership in the rest of the country. Their way was not as easy as that of today's visitors, as Celia Fiennes somewhat breathlessly reported, with little regard to punctuation, when she rode through the Peak by side-saddle in 1697.

All Derbyshire is full of steep hills, and nothing but the peakes of hills as thick as one by another is seen in most of the County which are very steepe which makes travelling tedious, and the miles long, you see neither hedge nor tree but only low drye stone walls around some ground, else its only hills and dales as thick as you can imagine.

And what these brave travellers found when they got to the Peak was a remote and isolated land where old customs and traditions had been retained from time immemorial. It was a place where the old gods were still worshipped, and where ancient tales of murder and mystery were still vividly remembered as if they had happened only yesterday. Astonishingly, the modern visitor can still find persistent echoes of that today in the Peak, even in our pressurised, commercialised and cynical society.

It is now widely accepted that the popular and colourful custom of the annual dressing of village wells or springs, first recorded in its early seven-teenth-century revival at Tissington, has much earlier, pagan origins. Most 'primitive' cultures, especially those in fast-draining or waterless areas, will give thanks by way of alms and oblations to the spirits or deities which send them the life-giving gift of water.

The White Peak in eponymous raiment – a snowy scene looking towards Manners Wood from above Bakewell.

And that is precisely, even in its current refined and predominately Christianised form, what the well dressings which attract so many admiring visitors in the summer months, are all about. Water, in the form of springs or wells, was vitally important for the existence of the tightly-knit communities and their stock which won a precarious living on the unforgiving 1000-foot high, limestone plateau now known as the White Peak. That is where and why the original well dressings began, although this unique form of folk-art has today never been more popular and has now spread to many other villages and towns keen to become involved in what most participants believe is a harmless cultural and Christian celebration, but what is essentially a pagan rite.

The mysterious Castleton Garland ceremony held each year on Oak Apple Day (29 May) also echoes of earlier, perhaps more sinister, beginnings. The 'King' is paraded on horseback around the village streets, unseen under a huge framework covered in flowers, until he reaches the parish church, where the garland is hoisted up to the top of the church tower where it is left to wither and die.

But Garland Day is not known as 'Baby Night' by the older residents of the little medieval township at the head of the Hope Valley without good reason, for it was the night when the rules were thrown out of the window, and when the usual etiquettes and social conventions were largely forgotten. Nine months later, there was a significant boost in the birth rate of the town.

The fact that it is linked with the pagan Celtic festival of Beltane when the coming of summer after the long, cold months of winter, was celebrated and

8

The Castleton Garland Ceremony, with Peveril Castle in the background.

when, in some isolated valleys of the Dark Peak, Beltane fires are still lit on prominent hilltops as we shall see, is perhaps significant. Perhaps the garland represents a long-forgotten welcome to the birth of a time of fruitfulness and fecundity, and the long-awaited death of the cold, hard months of winter.

Many tales of murder and mayhem still haunt the Peak District hills, and despite the lack of any historical evidence in most cases, those stories are still repeated and believed today. Lud's Church, a dark and dank chasm among the trees of Back Forest near the Staffordshire Roaches, is said to be the scene of the grisly beheading denouement of the classic early medieval Arthurian alliterative poem, *Sir Gawain and the Green Knight*. It was also the scene of a murder when soldiers raided a service being held in the remote 'church' by followers of John Wycliffe.

Places bearing the name of Robin Hood the mythical medieval outlaw and his loyal sidekick Little John, are abundant in the Peak District, especially around Hathersage, the alleged birth and burial place of 'John Little'. Standing as it does between his legendary haunts of Sherwood Forest in Nottinghamshire and Barnsdale in Yorkshire, the hills of the Peak could well have echoed to the sound of Robin's hunting horn.

Another example is the Battle of Win Hill, said to have taken place at some time in the Dark Ages of the seventh century, between the forces of Cuicholm, king of Wessex and Edwin, king of Northumbria. Embroiled in a dispute over land boundaries, Cuicholm had sent an envoy to the court of Edwin with instructions to murder the king. However, the plot was foiled by the heroic intervention of Lilla, one of Edwin's chief thane, who died as a result of his wounds, and is commemorated by Lilla Cross high on the North York Moors.

Intent on revenge, Edwin marched south and reached the Peak where Cuicholm had amassed a huge army which was swelled by the forces of Penda, the king of Mercia, another implacable enemy of Edwin. The two opposing armies camped overnight on the twin hills which guard the entrance to the Edale valley, and when they met the following day, somewhere near the present Townhead Bridge, the River Noe, in the manner of rivers featuring in Dark Age battlefields, was said to have run red with the blood of the fallen warriors.

Local tradition has it that Edwin's winning forces had camped on 'Win' Hill the night before, while Cuicholm's losers, had chosen 'Lose' Hill, so the result was really a foregone conclusion. Despite the fact that placename evidence tells us that Win Hill gets its name from the withies (an old name for rowans) which still grow upon it, and Lose Hill (pronounced 'loose') means the hill of the pig sties, local people still seem to prefer the old story.

The Dark Peak – looking towards Derwent Edge.

The remote and windswept hills and moors of the Peak District are rich in tales of murder and mystery, just as they have kept the secrets of the old ways. Just up the road from Win and Lose Hills is the mini Cheddar Gorge of the Winnats Pass, the old western route into the village of Castleton and the scene of the dreadful murder of Allan and Clara in the mid-eighteenth century.

No one knew, or were telling, who the murderers were, but the grisly fate of the five suspects speaks of some form of divine retribution. A similar fate awaited Anthony Lingard, the Wardlow Mires murderer, who was the last to swing from a gibbet in the county near the spooky butte of Peter's Stone.

As you might suspect, such tales of violent death and retribution have spawned a host of ghost stories in the Peak, ranging from the Grey Lady of the Castle Hotel in Castleton, to the many stories related to 'T'owd Man', as the spirits of long-dead lead miners are still known. Nowhere are these stories more graphically felt than in the evocative remains of Magpie Mine, high on the limestone plateau near Sheldon, where three miners met their untimely deaths in the nineteenth century after a long-running dispute over the right to work an underground vein.

The most haunted house in the Peak is said to be the delightfully-contradictory sixteenth-century Highlow Hall, near Abney. This was one of the famous Eyre halls, built by Robert, the founder of the famous Peakland line, for his seven sons, all in prominent positions where each could be seen from the other.

Son Nicholas had a short temper, and ruthlessly murdered a mason

11

whom he had employed and whom he apparently caught loitering on the job. The ghost of the workman at Highlow dates at least from the fourteenth century, and is one of the earliest to be recorded in the district. The most famous ghost of Highlow is however the White Lady, who has been consistently seen walking the corridors or across the courtyard of the house. She is said to be the spirit of a lady who was viciously murdered in an upstairs bedroom and then dragged along the landing and down the stairs.

And not all Peakland ghosts are ancient. Many people claim to have seen and heard a ghostly Avro Lancaster bomber from the Second World War zooming at low level over the waters of the Derwent Reservoir in the Upper Derwent Valley. This was where the crews of 617 Squadron – the Dambusters – trained in their specially-adapted Lancasters before their epic raid on the Ruhr dams in 1943. And nearby among the trees which surround the reservoir are the scarcely visible remains of the 'ghost village' of Tintown, or Birchinlee, where the navvies who built the dams lived and died for fifteen short years, before moving on to other projects across the country.

The Dark Peak moors have long been the graveyard for many aircraft which have been deceived by the frequent cloud and mists which so often obscure their boggy summits. The wreckage of a B-29 Superfortress 'Over Exposed', which crashed on Higher Shelf Stones on Bleaklow in 1943 killing all 13 crew members, was later the scene of a ghostly apparition after the finding of the dead pilot's wedding ring.

I've never knowingly seen a ghost myself, but on more than one occasion in certain places in the Peak, and I'm thinking of Lud's Church, on Peter's Stone, at Magpie or Odin Mines or on Higher Shelf Stones, the hairs on the back of my neck have stood up on end and I have sensed a feeling of unease, as the presence of an indefinable 'something' has made itself felt. Many people have said they have felt the same sensation while walking around the 'Plague Village' of Eyam – scene of the tragic yet heroic 'visitation' in the mid-seventeenth century.

Edward Browne's 'strange, mountainous, misty, moorish, rocky, wild country' continues to fascinate the estimated 22 million visitors who now flock annually into what later became Britain's first and most popular national park. This book retells the stories of some of the mysteries and murders which still haunt its everlasting hills and dales. Whether you believe them or not is in the end a matter for you, but either way, they make fascinating and often spinechilling reading.

CHAPTER TWO
The Old Religion

Tucked away unobtrusively over an archway in Buxton's excellent little museum on Terrace Road is a curious collection of stones carved with strange symbols and letters which were found by a local vicar near a Bronze Age barrow at Little Hadfield in 1846.

There are about ten carved stones, some apparently with typically-Celtic, bulging eye style heads, all taken from tree-topped Mouselow Hill, just outside Glossop. The 'low' element of the placename, deriving from the Old English 'hlaw', is significant because invariably in the Peak District, it refers to a burial mound or barrow.

The caption under the stones explains that they are thought to be of pre-Roman, Celtic Iron Age date, and that they may have belonged to larger groups of carvings 'of cult significance'. A guidebook of 1905 had described the stones thus: 'Some of the symbols have been recognised as representing the river of life, the wind blowing from the four quarters of the earth, Thoth, one of their gods (sic) and other objects which they worshipped.'

But when the stones were moved from the museum back to Mouselow Hill for a special exhibition linked to a three-year archaeological excavation in 1985, a series of strange and inexplicable events were eventually to lead to the temporary halting of the dig.

The archaeologist in charge received a series of anonymous phone calls which repeatedly asked why they were digging there, and warning of 'horned figures' and mentioning 'the Old Ways'. The local people who came to the on-site exhibition were obviously uneasy about the presence of the stones, some even claiming that they were 'evil'.

When the dig was eventually resumed, every member of the archaeological team suffered an unexpected injury involving loss of blood on the site. It was only after their leader had made a special visit to the hilltop in the darkness of the eve of the Celtic festival of Beltane on 1 May and dramatically announced from the centre of the dig that the spirits had nothing to fear from them, that the phone calls and harassment stopped.

Experts now believe that the stones had once formed part of a religious shrine which was still being used by some local people who followed the old religion, and who believed that the archaeological dig and attendant publicity would expose them.

The Celtic expert Dr Anne Ross was well aware of the ancient Celtic tradition which still existed in some parts of the Dark Peak, and suggested that the archaeologists had stumbled on the local tradition attached to the hill and the stones. The three Celtic heads originally included in the Mouselow Stones collection were thought to be highly significant.

The mysterious civilisation which is now known collectively as Celtic is well known for its veneration of the human head. Warriors often cut off the heads of their enemies beaten in battle and put them on poles outside their homes or carried them around their horses' necks as somewhat grisly trophies of war. They believed that the human spirit lived in the head, and by displaying the heads, they could prove they had captured not only the body but the spirit of their adversaries.

One tradition has it that the 'ball' used in today's riotous Shrove Tuesday Football Game at Ashbourne was originally the head of a defeated enemy, used in a sacrificial rite to commemorate victory in a hard-fought battle. If true, it gives a whole new significance to the phrase, 'On me 'ead, son'.

Celtic-style stone heads are a not uncommon sight in the Pennines, whether incorporated into the fabric of churches or on farmhouses or walls. There are some grotesque examples among the magnificent collection of Saxon and medieval carved stones in the porch of Bakewell's All Saints' parish church. They can usually be identified as stated above by their staring, bulging eyes, curly hair, occasional horns and gaping mouths.

The strange thing is that although these disembodied heads originally date from as far back as the Iron Age – perhaps 2000 years ago – they were still being carved on gateposts or in drystone walls in some of the more remote parts of the Pennines as late as the nineteenth century. And a BBC documentary broadcast in 1977 claimed that these stone heads were still being carved and buried in sacred places even today by some followers of the old ways. The old religion, it appears, is still alive and well in the remote hills and dales of the Peak.

Other traditions exposed by Dr Ross in the BBC Chronicle documentary centred on Longdendale, the gloomy, west-east valley of the River Etherow between Bleaklow and Black Hill, now apparently tamed and filled by reservoirs, power pylons and threaded by the roaring traffic of the A628 trunk road, and also now by the Longdendale Trail along the line of the former Woodhead railway line. Significantly, Mouselow Hill, or Castle (there is also evidence of a Norman motte and bailey castle on the site), stands like a

A Green Man in the Chapter House of Southwell Minster.

Early Christian Saxon preaching cross in Bakewell churchyard.

Carved heads can still be found in many Peak District gardens and homes.

Grotesque, Celtic-style stone heads in the south porch at Bakewell church.

15

guardian at the eastern entrance to the deep, trans-Pennine trench of Longdendale.

Dr Ross also revealed that wells and springs in the valley were still being decorated with bunches of flowers on the ancient festival dates, an echo of the still extant custom of the 'dressing' wells or springs as a thanksgiving to the gods for the gift of water on the White Peak limestone plateau, already mentioned. Although adopted in most cases today to carry mainly Christian or biblical themes, there can surely be no doubt of their primitive, pagan origins.

The same applies to the Castleton Garland ceremony, which takes place on Oak Apple Day (29 May) each year in the popular tourist village at the head of the Hope Valley. The garland-crowned King and his Queen process through the village to the special Garland tune, which may have been brought to Derbyshire by Cornish lead miners, as it bears a strong resemblance to that of the Cornish Floral Dance. The words of the tune reflect the long-held feeling of superiority which the people of Castleton have towards those of neighbouring Bradwell, whom they regarded as slaves of the Romans from the nearby fort of Navio between the two villages:

> Aa dunna know, Aa dunna care,
> What they do in Bradda (Bradwell).
> Piece o'beef and an old cow's yead (head),
> And a puddin' baked in a lantern.

After the tour of the village (including calls at every pub), the heavy, wooden-framed garland is finally hoisted to the top of St Edmund's parish church tower, where it is left to wither and die. Folklorists believe that although the ceremony is nowadays linked to the Restoration of Charles II in its date and the costumes of the King and Queen, it is more likely to orginally have been a pagan celebration linked to the coming of spring and the Celtic festival of Beltane, later 'sanitised' by the church.

Dr Ross also discovered that on the festival of Beltane (1 May), bonfires were still being lit on some farms, on hilltops, or on prominent stones, in the Dark Peak area. Further south on the Staffordshire Roaches, May Day saw sheep being ceremonially herded around the Bawd Stone, a 20-ton boulder balanced on three legs of stone on the slopes of Hen Cloud. Sick or infirm local people processed to this anciently-venerated feature in the landscape from as far away as Leek to be healed. Some standing stones, like the Bawd Stone, were whitewashed by unseen worshippers annually on the eve of May Day.

Belief in the powers of a powerful mother goddess, sometimes known as

Anu, and a male horned god was also found to be still strong in some of these isolated communities. We have already met the Celtic goddess Arn or Anu, who is commemorated by St Anne's Well at Buxton, one of the original seventeenth-century Wonders of the Peak and after whom the Romans originally named their town. And another of the Wonders, Mam Tor, the so-called 'Shivering Mountain' dominating the head of the Hope Valley above Castleton, is thought to have a similar Celtic origin, meaning 'Mother Mountain'.

Belief in the old Celtic gods is reflected in other place-names of the Peak District. Hob was the common local name for a mischievous spirit who usually lived in woodland, hurst being the Old English name for a wood or forest. Variously known as Hob Hurst or Hob i' th' Hurst, this capricious wood elf was thought to live in or near ancient stone circles, tumuli or other solitary places.

Local folk would refuse to go near such places at certain times for fear of upsetting Hob. When Hob was irritated, he could make a farmer's cows go dry, the milk turn sour or even shatter the crockery in the farmhouse. But when he was in a good mood, he would ensure that the cows gave plenty of milk, cause the cream to churn quickly into butter, assist at calving time, and even increase the supply of the vital hay needed to feed the stock through the winter months.

The crumbling limestone landslip known as Hob Hurst's House stands high above Monsal Dale and below the Iron Age hillfort of Fin Cop. A giant named Hob was alleged to have lived here, and a skeleton of early British date was found among the shattered rocks. The escarpment above which dominates the classic view from Monsal Head is known locally as the Great Finn and could take its name from the Celtic 'fin' meaning white or clear, or the Old English 'fin' for a stack of wood, perhaps a beacon, or does it remember a giant by the name of Finn like the Irish god Fionn MacCummail?

There's another Hob Hurst's House at over 1000 feet above the sea on the East Moor on the edge of Bunker's Hill Wood just north of Harland Edge. This is an unusual barrow or burial mound dating from the Bronze Age surrounded by an almost square ditch and embankment. Like so many of the Peak District's barrows, it has a large crater in the top of it, evidence of the work of that indefatigable barrow digger Thomas Bateman, who excavated the mound on 3 June, 1853.

Fortunately, he left one of his most evocative descriptions of the opening of the barrow, when he discovered a deposit of calcined human bones 'lying in the very spot where they had been drawn together while the embers of the funeral pyre were glowing,' some pieces of charcoal and two lumps of burnt lead ore. In his classic *Ten Years' Diggings in Celtic & Saxon Grave Hills* (1861), Bateman attempted to explain the name:

In the popular name given to the barrow, we have an indirect testimony to its great antiquity, as Hobhurst's House signifies the abode of an unearthly or supernatural being, accustomed to haunt woods and other solitary places, respecting whom many traditions yet linger in remote villages. Such an idea could only arise in a superstitious age long ago, yet sufficiently modern to have effaced all traditionary recollection of the original intention of the mound; it likewise affords a curious instance of the inherent tendency of the mind to assign a reason for everything uncommon or unaccountable, which no extent of ignorance or apathy seems able totally to eradicate.

And he added the perceptive thought:

Many of the remaining prehistoric monuments of our land are similarly connected with names well known in popular mythology, now so rapidly vanishing, that it is probable the legends will be forgotten, while the names alone will be perpetuated as long as the structures with which they are identified exist.

Yet another Hob lived at Thirst or Hurst's House Cave in Deepdale, south of King's Sterndale. Nearby is a spring which Hob is supposed to have blessed, and which is said to have curative properties for those who bathe in it on Good Friday.

Springs, marshy places and pools were venerated by the Celts as windows into the twilight world of the Afterlife. Human sacrifices, such as that of Lindow Man found in a peat bog at Lindow Moss near Mobberley in Cheshire in 1984 and now in the British Museum, were often made in such places. Like many other 'bog bodies', the Lindow Man underwent the ritual triple death common in Celtic human sacrifice – he was pole-axed, garrotted and drowned. Dr Annie Ross has speculated that he may have been a Druidic prince sacrificed to the Gods as the Roman empire gradually set about exterminating the last vestiges of the old, pagan religion.

Other reminders of the old gods are found in the place-names of a couple of settlements on the White Peak plateau. Friden, high on the limestone plateau, was previously known as Frigdene and takes its name from Freya or Frig, the Norse goddess of fertility and the equivalent to the Celtic Brigid or Bride. Nearby is Wensley which takes its name from Woden, the pre-eminent Saxon god who also gave his name to Wednesday (Woden's Day). Thor, the Norse god of thunder, gave his name to the archetypal cave man's dwelling which yawns out impressively from its 300-foot high crag over the

Manifold Valley in Staffordshire, while Odin Mine, near Castleton, said to be the oldest lead mine in the Peak (first recorded in 1280), gets its name from the chief of the Norse gods, who is associated with death, wisdom, magic and madness (see Chapter 7).

Odin Mine has an evil reputation among cavers, and there are stories of its being haunted by the ghost of one of the murderers in the Allan and Clara case (see Chapter 4), and of its being the scene of a disaster in which 70 lead miners were drowned after a landslip. All I know is that when I made an exploration of the mine with members of the Masson Caving Group in 1998, I couldn't get out fast enough. There was certainly a sense of malevolent foreboding about the place.

Unlikely as it may seem being so far from the sea, there are several legends linked to mermaids inhabiting Peak District pools. Perhaps the best-known is that haunting the dark, reed-fringed acidic tarn known as Mermaid's Pool, which lies under the western shoulder of the Peak's highest point, the forbidding 2000-foot (600m) plateau of Kinder Scout.

The story goes that a beautiful mermaid lives in a cave on the side of Kinder and comes out every day to bathe in the pool. And the legend is that if you are lucky enough to see her perform her chilly ablutions on Easter Eve, you will be granted immortality. Before you scoff at such an unlikely occurrence, perhaps you should remember the story of the retired soldier Aaron Ashton of nearby Hayfield, who was a frequent visitor to the Mermaid's Pool and died in 1835 at the ripe old age of 104.

Many visitors have felt a sense of melancholy, even malevolence, about this desolate spot – although my fondest memory of a visit there is during the severe winter of 1977/78. We'd trekked up through deepening snow from Hayfield to view the increasingly-rare sight of Kinder Downfall frozen into a 100-foot shimmering curtain of ice, and on our way back, called to look at the ice-covered Mermaid's Pool. We could hardly believe what we saw, but the side of the pool was a perfectly-constructed igloo, presumably made by some enterprising ramblers from blocks of frozen snow. No mermaid perhaps, but I must admit that we half expected to encounter Eskimo Nell!

Over on the Staffordshire side of the Peak lie two other moorland pools associated with mermaids. The circular pool known as Blake Mere lies close to the Mermaid Inn high on the Staffordshire moors east of Leek, and is thought to be bottomless.

A poem preserved in the pub warns visitors not to be tempted if the mermaid appears:

A misty view of the Mermaid's Pool from the western edge of Kinder Scout.

> *She calls on you to greet her,*
> *Combing her dripping crown,*
> *And if you go to meet her,*
> *She ups and drags you down.*

Visible from the pool and not far away across the Leek-Buxton road lies the serrated skyline of Ramshaw Rocks and the Roaches, some of the most spectacular rock scenery to be found anywhere in the Peak.

Situated at over 1500 feet on the Roaches ridge, with its far-reaching views across the Cheshire Plain, lies another dark, deep peaty pool known as Doxey Pool, which harbours another legend of a mermaid. This one has a name – Jenny Greenteeth – and she has an equally fiercesome reputation as her counterpart over at Blake Mere. The two murky pools are said to be connected, so perhaps it is the same mermaid, and both share the legend that they never seem to increase or decrease in size, and no birds are supposed to fly over them.

CELTIC FESTIVALS

The festivals celebrated by the ancient Celtic people of the Peak District are long established, and coincided with key moments in the farming calendar. The chief festivals, many of which have since been adopted by Christianity, are:-

Samhain, 1 November, the end of summer and the festival of the dead (Hallowe'en)

Imbolc, 1 February, the time of the lactation of the ewes (the Old Christmas Day)

Beltane, 1 May, marking the beginning of summer (May Day)

Lughnasa, 1 August, the beginning of the harvest (Lammas Day or Harvest Festival)

ᘓᗺᘎ

CHAPTER THREE

Arthur and Robin

I'll never forget my first visit nearly thirty years ago to Lud's Church, the mysterious chasm hidden deep in the old oaks and birches of Back Forest, north of the Roaches in the Staffordshire Moorlands. We were on a pilgrimage to find the fabled Green Chapel where Sir Gawain had faced his epic showdown with the Green Knight in the classic early fourteenth-century alliterative poem, *Sir Gawain and the Green Knight*.

It was a dark and damp autumnal day with mists wreathing the trees as we descended from Roach End towards the valley of the Black Brook. Like Gawain and his guide, we had travelled:

By bluffs where boughs were bare they passed,
Climbed by cliffs where the cold clung:
Under the high clouds, ugly mists
Merged damply with the moors and melted on the mountains.

Like theirs, our 'way through the woods was wonderfully wild', and the last burnished gold beech leaves clung stubbornly to the branches as we walked down across a lemon carpet of fallen larch needles towards the junction of the Black Brook with the River Dane at Forest Bottom. Like Gawain, we followed the directions to:

Ride down this rough track round yonder cliff
Till you arrive in a rugged ravine at the bottom,
Then look about on the flat, on your left hand,
And you will view there in the vale that very chapel,
And the grim gallant who guards it always.

Now we climbed up on the Victorian engineered path up through the dripping birchwoods above the Dane until the weird, contorted shapes of Castle Cliff Rocks appeared out of the mists to our right...

Great crooked crags, cruelly jagged;
The bristling barbs of rocks seemed to brush the sky...

Eventually, after some searching, we found the concealed entrance to Lud's

Could this be the Green Knight? Strange rock sculpture in Lud's Church.

Church, then blocked by a massive fallen slab of rock:

> *It had a hole in each end and on either side,*
> *And was overgrown with grass in great patches.*
> *All hollow it was within, only an old cavern*
> *Or the crevice of an ancient crag.*

At last we had found the setting where most academics seem to agree the anonymous author of the poem had Gawain submitting to a blow from the axe of the dread-locked Green Knight as he had promised that he would. This was after Arthur's favourite had accepted the challenge and struck off the head of the mythical figure in Arthur's Christmastide court exactly twelve months before.

Once inside the dog-legged cavern, which is actually a huge landslip, the overall impression was of greenness – dark, dank and dripping greenness. Grass, moss and ferns clung tenaciously to the vertical sides of the 50-foot deep ravine, while trees overhung the top, adding to the all-pervading gloom. As Edward Bradbury recorded in 1881:

> *Young ash-trees and hazels form a roof of luminous green, rare plants and ferns*
> *and dwarf trees spring from every cleft; cool mosses robe the naked rocks; high up*
> *in a hazardous interstice a hawk has built its nest.*

Although we didn't see the hawk, as we cautiously picked our way across the slippery boulders which littered the floor of the chasm, I think we were half-expecting to come across the legendary giant face-to-face, striding out of the mists 'garbed all in green'.

Then, taking one last look back as we left the claustrophobic confines of the cavern, we suddenly saw the unmistakeable craggy outline of the giant's head in the rock wall above. A great, lantern jaw and grim, beetled brows encased in a visor-clad helmet frowned down on the dismal scene. And to cap it all, a holly tree sprouted out of the living rock above – and we remembered that the Green Knight had entered Arthur's court carrying a bough of holly.

It was a strangely eerie moment, seeing this rock-carved face appear before us just as our thoughts had been straying towards the legendary figure. But perhaps that's why we saw him.

It was Prof. Ralph Elliott then of Keele University who in 1958 conclusively proved that *Sir Gawain and the Green Knight*, perhaps the greatest medieval English poem outside the work of Geoffrey Chaucer, was not only set in Staffordshire but was in all probability written by a local poet. Writing in an article in *The Times*, he claimed that the author's use of the north-

Midland dialect and the 'sensuous vividness of his landscape painting' of the north Staffordshire countryside meant that he had 'both a remarkable eye for detail and a close familiarity with the scenes depicted.'

The melodramatic story of Sir Gawain and the Green Knight echoes the old Celtic belief in the power of the head, and the beheading game described in the story is a common one in Celtic mythology. The name of Lud's Church is perhaps also significant, because some authorities claim that it is taken from Lugh or Lud, the sun and sky god of the Celts and the husband of Anu who gave his name to the Festival of Lughnasa (1 August or Lammas Day) when farmers traditionally traded their stock.

More likely, however, it was named after Walter de Lud-Auk, a Lollard preacher who was a follower of John Wycliffe and who held services during the early fifteenth century in the remote natural chapel to avoid the prying eyes of the authorities. Legend has it that soldiers, attracted by the singing at one of these services, raided the illicit ceremony and Walter's beautiful grand daughter Alice was accidentally killed by a stray bullet. Later, a white figurehead known as Alice decorated a niche high in the walls of the cavern, but this actually came from local landlord Sir Philip Brocklehurst's ship, the *Nimrod*, which was used for Antarctic exploration and which is also remembered in the Ship Inn at nearby Wincle.

Another Arthurian legend associated with the western side of the Peak District is the legend of the Wizard at Alderley Edge, the wooded escarpment which overlooks the Cheshire Plain near Wilmslow. Alderley Edge is a strange place, honeycombed with old copper, cobalt and lead mine workings which may date back as far as the Bronze Age, if the evidence of a crude wooden spade found in one of the tunnels is to be believed. The Legend of Alderley, according to local author Alan Garner who was told it by his grandfather, relates to a farmer from Mobberley who was taking a milk-white mare for sale at Macclesfield Fair.

As he reached the cave known as Thieves' Hollow on Alderley Edge, he was approached by an old bearded man who said he wanted to buy the horse from him. The farmer thought he could get a better price at the fair, so he refused the sale.

Of course, the farmer failed to sell the horse at Macclesfield, and on the way home, met up with the old man again by Thieves' Hollow. He agreed the sale and then was led to Stormy Point, where the old man struck the rock with his staff. Miraculously, the rock opened up, and the farmer was led inside through a pair of iron gates into a cave where slept a king with 149 of his knights all in silver armour, alongside their 148 white horses. The farmer's white horse was obviously needed to make up the number.

The astonished farmer was paid for his horse with golden treasure and then taken back to the iron gates which closed behind him. Try as he might, he could never find those gates into the underworld again.

The sleeping knights myth is a common one in Britain, and is a legend Alderley Edge shares with Lliwedd on Snowdon and Sewingshields Crags on Hadrian's Wall. The king is usually identified as Arthur, waiting to come to Britain's rescue with his knights of the Round Table in time of national disaster, and the wizard is, of course, none other than his faithful sage and mentor, Merlin.

Along with the inevitable stories of hauntings by headless figures at Lud's Church, another of the many stories associated with it claims it as a hiding place for the legendary outlaw Robin Hood. Some people have linked the Green Knight with Robin Goodfellow and Jack o'the Green or the Green Man – the spirit of the woods and the physical personification of Nature.

But one thing is sure and that is that the Peak District is not short of links with the legendary medieval outlaw who may, in the last analysis, have been nothing more than some kind of universal medieval superhero, along the lines of Superman or Spiderman.

Many words have been expended on the quest to identify an actual historical person who was the model for the dashing outlaw, who traditionally robbed the rich to pay the poor. The fact is that there were many Robin Hoods, or Robehodes, and it became a popular surname for a commoner who strayed outside the law during the early Middle Ages. One historically-recorded instance was Piers Venables, a Derbyshire man who in true Robin Hood style rescued a prisoner from Tutbury Castle in 1439 and, it was said, gathered round him a gang of men 'beyng of his clothing, and in manere be Robyn Hode and his meynee.' Whatever the truth about the elusive hero, as a seventeenth-century commentator said, he was 'no fox that hath only one hole.'

The first mention of the name of Robin Hood appears to have been in William Langland's *Vision of Piers the Plowman* which was written about 1377, and is one of the earliest pieces of English literature to have survived:

I do not know my paternoster perfectly as the priest sings it,
But I know the rhymes of Robin Hood and Randolph, Earl of Chester.

This seems to indicate that the rhymes of Robin Hood must have been quite well known and in general circulation by the end of the fourteenth century.

Most authorities now seem to believe that all the well-loved modern stories about the man in Lincoln green seem to stem from a group of popular ballads which were circulated by strolling players who toured the halls of the feudal overlords at the time. Of these, the first seems to be Robin Hood and the Monk dating from about 1450, and Robin Hood and the Potter probably written shortly after 1503. But perhaps the best-known of these collections of ballads came from the press of the famous English printer Wynken de Worde, who worked between 1492 and 1534 and published *A Lyttell Geste of Robyn Hode*, a poem of 456 four-line stanzas divided into eight cantos or 'fyttes'. It is from these tales told by strolling players that most of the Robin Hood legends so beloved of Hollywood film makers and tourist boards, originate.

But whatever and whoever the popular outlaw was, he is remembered in the Peak District by a string of place-names which have led some over-enthu-siastic supporters to claim his birthright from his traditional and better-known 'homes' in Sherwood, Nottinghamshire and Barnsdale, South Yorkshire.

Probably the best-known is Robin Hood's Stride, the dramatic natural gritstone tor near Birchover which is said to be the length of his stride. He must have been a giant as well as an outlaw, because the distance between the two eroded pinnacles is around 66ft or 20 metres! The alternative name for the outcrop above the ancient Portway packhorse route is Mock Beggar's Hall, from its resemblance in certain light to a ruined building. The two pinnacles are known to climbers as the Weasel and the Inaccessible – which the ancient graffiti carved upon it over the years proves it certainly is not.

Just across the Portway and hidden behind a venerable, spreading yew at the foot of Cratcliffe Tor is the Hermit's Cave, where an elaborate crucifix thought to date from the fourteenth century is carved in the rock of the back wall. The place was obviously once the home of a clerical hermit – could it have been Friar Tuck? There is certainly an air of mystery about this place – a favourite playground of my children when they were younger. And yes, Robin Hood was among the games they played around these rocks.

Robin Hood's Picking Rods are two isolated standing stones set in a gritstone base on Ludworth Moor (there is that name again) near Glossop and close to the Cheshire border. Once known as the Maiden Stones, their modern name has suggested to those of a vivid imagination that they were used by Robin to bend his bows as he strung them. A more likely theory is that they were originally boundary stones or the base of preaching crosses, although why two are mounted into a socketed base remains unexplained.

Also to be found on the moors of the Peak District are Robin Hood's Stoop on Offerton Moor, and both Robin Hood's and Little John's Wells are

Robin Hood's Stride, or Mock Beggar's Hall, near Birchover.

on the National Trust's Longshaw Estate. Nearby too is Robin Hood's Cave, a natural balcony in the escarpment of Stanage Edge, with wonderful views across the Derwent Valley. Although pretty well known to the climbing fraternity as a picnic spot, the Rev. M.F.H. Hulbert, former vicar of Hathersage, claimed in his booklet *Little John of Hathersage* that:

> *Hikers can pass within a few feet above and below it in hundreds every summer weekend and never know of its existence. The series of interconnecting caves and passages is very well concealed. They can be reached from the top and come out halfway down the face of the cliff giving panoramic views for miles to the south and west. Pools of water can always be found nearby so that anyone in hiding could survive for long periods, and the formation of the caves means they could easily be defended by one man against a large number of attackers. In just such a place an outlaw might hide for months undetected, if the need arose.*

Robin Hood's Moss and Robin Hood's Croft, an old sheep shelter, are also marked on maps of the moors surrounding the Derwent Dams in the Upper Derwent Valley, and there is a Robin Hood's Cross, probably another boundary marker, on Abney Moor.

But it is Little John, the bluff, plain-speaking giant of a man who was Robin's most faithful lieutenant, who has most associations with the Peak District. Originally called John Little, he was supposedly a nailor from Hathersage, where that trade had been practised for hundreds of years, and he is said to be buried in the famous grave by the parish church door. There is also a Little John public house, complete with an imaginative sign of Little John fighting Robin with quarterstaffs, in Station Road.

Much is made of the Little John connection in St Michael's church in Hathersage, where you can buy souvenirs featuring Little John from erasers to metal badges. The 'grave', between two heavily-clipped yews, is about 10ft (3m) long, which would seem to indicate that a very large person was buried there. It is railed-off and decked with flowers, and now appropriately cared for by the Ancient Order of Foresters.

There are stories that during the eighteenth century, a local dignitary opened the grave to prove once and for all that it marked the last resting place of the fabled outlaw. Six feet below the surface a huge thigh bone was discovered and found to measure 32in (about a metre). It was returned to the grave after a series of unfortunate accidents.

However, more recent research by Prof. Brian Robinson claims that the so-called 'grave' is actually the site of the official measure of the Hathersage village perch – a unit of measurement which was used during the Middle

Ages. The two small stones just visible at the head and foot of the 'grave' measure 10ft 9ins, which is close to the measurement by which the old 'short acre' of 3240 square yards was calculated.

Incidentally, the length of the local perch was settled by some pretty arbitrary methods in those days, one of which involved the use of 16 men as they left the village church at the end of a Sunday service. They were stood in a row, foot-to-foot behind one another, the total length of their feet being designated as the length of the local perch.

Further alleged proof that Hathersage was Little John's home was that, until the middle of the eighteenth century, a 79in spliced yew bow, some arrows, a fragment of chain metal armour and a green cap hung in the church and were pointed out to wondering visitors as belonging to Little John. The great bow and the armour were later removed from the church and taken to Cannon Hall, near Barnsley 'for safe keeping'. It was said that in 1715, a certain Captain Naylor strung the ancient bow and shot a deer with it. It took a pull of 160lbs to draw the massive bow.

Little John's cottage (now gone) also once stood at the east end of the church, overlooking the valley of – appropriately – the Hood Brook.

Of course we will never know the truth about whether or not there ever was a real Robin Hood and Little John. It is hard to give total credence to two mainly fictional characters for whom, in the last analysis, there is no conclusive historical evidence. But if the evidence of local place-names and legends are anything to go by, the Peak District must have as strong a claim as Nottinghamshire or Yorkshire – although whether their respective tourist boards would agree about that is another matter.

A PEAKLAND ROBIN HOOD DIRECTORY

Robin Hood Locations

Robin Hood's Cave, Stanage Edge SK244837.

Robin Hood's Well, Longshaw SK266801.

Robin Hood's Cross, Abney SK 182803.

Robin Hood's Stoop, Offerton SK217806.

Robin Hood's Spring, Howden Moors SK193932.

Robin Hood's Moss, Howden Moors SK195935.

Robin Hood Hamlet, near Hathersage.

Robin Hood Hamlet, Chesterfield/Baslow road SK279721.

Robin Hood Public House, Chesterfield/Baslow road SK279721.

Robin Hood's Croft, Lead Hill, Derwent Valley SK197867.

Robin Hood's Table, Barbrook Valley SK277755.

Robin Hood's Stride, near Birchover SK223623.

Robin Hood's Picking Rods, Rowarth SK010912.

Robin Hood's Chair, Hope Dale.

Robin Hood's Leap, Chatsworth.

Little John Locations

Little John's Grave, Hathersage Churchyard SK231815.

Little John's Well, Longshaw SK266795.

Little John Hotel, Hathersage.

CHAPTER FOUR

Murder and Revenge

This wild ravine is bounded on each side by perpendicular rocks of an amazing height, yet it is not wholly devoid of beauty; numbers of rare and elegant plants picturesquely adorn the steepy sides of this, in other respects, deep, lone, and dreary pass.

This early twentieth-century description of the Winnats Pass, to the west of the tourist honeypot of Castleton at the head of the Hope Valley, reflects the contemporary view of natural scenery – something to be endured rather than enjoyed.

The name comes from the Old English wind geats, which translates as 'the pass through which the wind sweeps' – an entirely apt description of the limestone gorge through which the westerly winds are often funnelled to blast out over the medieval planned township at its feet and down the sylvan Hope Valley. As Edward Bradbury wrote in his In the Derbyshire Highlands of 1881:

The ravine presents a natural passage for the mountain winds that sweep through it and wail and moan and howl and scream; while its particular situation is such as to collect the breezes from each point of the compass. This rift is one of Nature's romantic openings in the mountain limestone. Narrow is the path between the perilous and precipitous crags.

In this land of caves memorably described by Sir Arthur Conan Doyle as 'a hollow country', the Winnats was for long explained in the guidebooks as a collapsed cave system. But that oft-repeated theory is now discredited by modern geomorphologists.

Dr Trevor Ford, doyen of Peak District geologists, says that the channel which we now know as the Winnats was initially formed on the northern edge of the tropical White Peak carboniferous lagoon, some 350 million years ago. A shallow channel was formed between belts of coral reefs, and swept clear by tides washing in and out twice a day. Later the channel was filled by the gritty shales of a river delta formed of the rocks which were later to become known as the Millstone Grit. Then, in the final shaping of the gorge, a rushing, corrosive meltwater stream from the retreating glaciers of the Ice Age sought out the weakness provided by the shale and re-excavated the channel to its present impressive depth.

The cave-filled hillsides of Treak Cliff and Long Cliff to the north and south of the Winnats are the steep outer faces of that incredibly-ancient reef limestone seascape. Treak Cliff, of course, is well known for its deposits of the rare Blue John fluorspar in its famous show caves, the Treak Cliff and Blue John Caverns. Long Cliff is honeycombed by mineral veins of lead and fluorspar, extensively worked by the old lead miners, who when they built a subterranean canal to drain the mine discovered the 'Bottomless Pit' of the Speedwell Mine, which was to become yet another of Castleton's show caves.

But our story concerns a grim tale of murder and revenge which took place in the Winnats during the spring of 1758. In mid-April of that year, according to a pamphlet published locally in Castleton at the turn of the last century, a well-to-do couple called at the Royal Oak Inn in Stoney Middleton to feed their horses. Their names were Allan and Clara, and as they waited for their horses, their hostess eavesdropped on their conversation.

It seemed that they had eloped against Clara's father's wishes, to get married in the parish church of King Charles, King and Martyr at Peak Forest, which was a kind of Derbyshire Gretna Green. By some quirk of ecclesiastical law, the incumbent of Peak Forest church did not demand

A wintry view of the Winnats Pass, near Castleton.

33

banns to be read in advance and could grant probate and marriage licences.

But Clara, the daughter of a nobleman, had experienced an awful premonition in a dream that they would die at the hands of assailants in a picturesque valley – a grim portent which was to prove chillingly accurate.

Allan, apparently a gentleman from the south of England, tried vainly to reassure his bride-to-be, and they set out for Castleton, where they intended to stop for a short while before setting out on the final stage of their fateful journey, up through the Winnats and then to Peak Forest via Eldon Hill and Sparrowpit.

They stopped at one of the inns in Castleton for breakfast, which they took in the parlour. In an adjacent room, a group of four uncouth lead miners were already the worse for wear for drink and were eventually evicted by the landlord, anxious to give the right impression to his more distinguished guests.

Picking up another friend en route, the miners went off on their drunken way to work at Odin Mine, one of the oldest lead mines in the area, but on the way they reflected on the heavy saddle bags being carried by the young gentleman and his young lady. They decided, in their drunken stupor, that there could be easy pickings if they were intercepted in the Winnats, which is what they resolved to do.

The couple left the inn and headed towards the gloomy portals of the gorge. Just as they entered the pass, the miners armed with pick axes leapt out on them, and Clara called out: 'Allan, my dream! my dream!' After imploring their assailants not to kill them, the terrified couple were led to a barn which stood near the site of the present entrance to Speedwell Cavern.

Realising that the couple were by now well known and would be missed if they did not appear at Peak Forest later that day, the miners resolved that they would have to be killed or their nefarious deed would be found out.

Allan appealed for the life of his loved one, but the miners knew they both had to die, and after a short consultation, they were clubbed to a bloody death by pick axes. The haul from this violent deed was £200 in money and valuables, which they decided to divide between them. The miners remained in the barn with the bodies of their innocent victims until night-fall, and resolved to come back at midnight to bury the bodies.

According to the pamphlet: 'Midnight came and they repaired to the solitary place; but their "blood guiltiness" peopled the shades of night with horrid forms! They heard in imagination the shrieks of woe, and they retreated from the dismal place. The following night they ventured again; but on arrival at the scene of blood, two steeds, each mounted by a spectre, with hair dabbled with gore, rushed past them, and entered the barn; on which they retraced their steps more terrified than before.'

Eventually on the third night they steeled themselves again and buried the bodies a short distance from the barn. As the miners suspected, the young couple were soon missed, and their horses were found, saddled and bridled, in the King's forest near the Winnats.

Local people immediately suspected the worst, imagining that the couple had been murdered and thrown into the apparently bottomless depths of nearby Eldon Hole, the largest open pothole in the Peak. But it was to be many years later before two bodies were found which were thought to be Allan and Clara, and were buried in St Edmund's churchyard at Castleton. But still the identity of their murderers remained a mystery. Until that is, a series of strange, apparently accidental, events pointed the finger at the five men who were responsible.

One of the miners bought horses with his share of the booty, but they all died in rapid succession, and he frequently said: 'I always have a beautiful lady with me – she rides on my horse.' The daughter of another of the miners was seen at church wearing a very rich silk dress, and people began to put two and two together.

Some years after the horrendous deed, one of the guilty men fell from a precipice in the Winnats and was killed instantly. Another was mysteriously killed by a falling stone in the same place, and a third lost his reason and died in a miserable state having tried to commit suicide on several occasions.

A fourth man was more successful in his death wish, and hanged himself. Finally, the horse-owning miner, after lying on his death bed for ten weeks, eventually owned up to the crime, and admitted that it was he and his four friends who had robbed, murdered and buried Allan and Clara in the Winnats. He added: 'She was the handsomest woman I ever saw,' just before he too died.

In the words of the pamphleteer: 'Though the hand of human justice did not reach these guilty beings, yet the hand of God found them out, even on earth'.

What is purported to be Clara's red Morocco leather saddle is on display at the Speedwell Cavern, a short distance from where the dreadful deed took place, having been purchased from the museum of the well-known Peakland antiquarian and barrow-digger, Thomas Bateman of Middleton-by-Youlgreave.

Peter's Stone is a strange, butte-like outcrop of limestone which stands sentinel at the northern entrance to Cressbrook Dale and is a prominent

Peter's Stone, Cressbrook Dale. It was near here that Antony Lingard was gibbeted.

landmark, for those who know where to look for it, on the A623 Stoney Middleton-Peak Forest road.

It is supposed to have taken its name from its similarity to the dome of St Peter's Cathedral in Rome, and although I'd known it for years, I'd never actually climbed this detached block, formed after an ancient landslip broke away from the crags behind.

One fine summer's evening after visiting a sick friend in the nearby village of Litton with my young son, Iain, I decided that the time had come to climb Peter's Stone – merely because I had the time and it was there.

We parked near the hamlet of Wardlow Mires, and as usual, Dad set off at far too fast a pace down the dale, with Iain trailing some way behind. I reached the grassy summit quite easily, after a little scramble up a fissure at the rear of the outcrop, and admired the view up the dale towards Tansley Dale and the distant wooded confines of Cressbrook Dale. I remember thinking it was strange that I hadn't seen Iain coming up the dale behind me.

I scrambled down the rock and started to look for him. I circled the outcrop, beginning to worry that he might have fallen, and calling out his name at the top of my voice. There was no sight nor sound of Iain and by now I was really concerned that something might have happened to him, and I cursed my impetuousness in racing ahead to climb the crag.

Several minutes passed as I searched for Iain round the rocks, and I was getting more and more worried and frustrated that I couldn't find him. Then he suddenly appeared in the col between the outcrop and the cliff behind, obviously upset and as distressed and worried as I was.

The astonishing thing was that he'd been doing exactly the same as me, walking round the rock calling out my name and imagining that I may have fallen and lay injured somewhere.

When I recounted this odd tale to my Litton friend, she said she wasn't at all surprised. 'It's a very strange place, and odd things can happen there,' she said.

I knew that the last public gibbeting in Derbyshire had taken place near Peter's Stone in the early nineteenth century, and that local people didn't like to walk there, especially late at night.

In fact, the gibbeting of twenty-one-year-old Antony Lingard of nearby Tideswell for the murder of the Wardlow Mires toll-keeper Hannah Oliver in 1815 was an important catalyst in the eventual banning of the barbarous punishment.

Strangely enough, Lingard was betrayed by his penchant for Hannah's fine pair of new red leather shoes. He stole the shoes from her lifeless body after he had strangled her on New Year's Day, 1815, for the takings from the tollhouse which she ran at Wardlow Mires. Hannah's body was found by travellers who could not raise her as they passed along the two turnpike roads which intersected at the Wardlow junction.

Apparantly, Lingard wanted to give the shoes to a girlfriend – supposedly pregnant by him – in Tideswell, but suspecting their origin she refused the offer. Eventually, Lingard disposed of the shoes in a haystack, but even then they haunted his fevered brain and he reclaimed them and foolishly kept them in his cottage.

There they were found by police investigating the murder. They consulted the local shoemaker, Samuel Marsden of Stoney Middleton, who recognised them as a pair he had made for Hannah. This was confirmed when he took one shoe apart and recovered a piece of packing he had put in it which bore the prophetic motto: 'Commit no crime'.

Lingard was arrested and tried at Derby, where he was found guilty and hanged on 8 March, 1815 and his body brought to the field still known as Gibbet Field by Peter's Stone, to be hung in chains as a grisly example to other wrongdoers.

As was the custom in those days, a sermon was due to be preached at the gibbet site and it so happened that John Longden, a Methodist minister who lived in the Woodlands Valley and later kept the Snake Inn, had walked the 15 miles across country to preach at Tideswell that day but found most of his congregation were at the gibbeting. Undeterred, he immediately set off for Wardlow and gave his sermon, which appropriately enough was a passionate exhortation to penitence.

In addition to the crowds of local people, tradesmen and hucksters had set up their stalls and tumblers and other entertainers kept the huge, ghoulish crowds amused. Subsequent toll-keepers at Wardlow Mires complained at the ghostly sound of Lingard's bones rattling in the wind in their iron cage, and the gibbet was not dismantled until 1826, when Lingard's pitiful remains were anonymously buried on the site.

But Longden was not the only person to be affected by the morbid sight of Lingard's decomposing body hung up for all to see. According to a famous poem by William Newton of Cressbrook, the so-called 'Minstrel of the Peak', one stormy night Lingard's father came upon the awful sight of his son's body swinging in the wind.

The poem, which is claimed to have given an important impetus to the campaign to ban gibbeting, has this somewhat theatrical title and introduction:

The supposed soliloquy of a Father under the Gibbet of his Son, upon one of the Peak mountains near Wardlow.

Time – Midnight   Scene – A Storm

> *Art thou, my Son, suspended here on high, –*
> *Ah! What a sight to meet a Father's eye!*
> *To see what most I prized, what most I loved,*
> *What most I cherished – and once most approved,*
> *Hung in mid air to feed the nauseous worm,*
> *And waving horrid in the midnight storm!*

But he concludes the rather melodramatic piece with an undisguised appeal to the legal authorities:

> *O ye who have life, or death, at your command,*
> *Deal the sad dole, if death, with lenient hands.*
> *If crime demand it, let the offender die,*
> *But let no more the Gibbet brave the sky;*
> *No more let vengeance on the dead be hurl'd,*
> *But hide the victim from a gazing world.*

Whether the poem had any effect at all is hard to say, but it was widely distributed and the vengeful practice of gibbeting was eventually banned in 1834 – nineteen years after the body of Antony Lingard had swung in the breeze near the spooky sentinel of Peter's Stone.

ɘχ

PLACES OF EXECUTION

Placenames are often a good clue to what went on in the past, and although not everywhere with the words gib or hanging in their names indicate a place of execution, many, such as the Gibbet Field at Wardlow, do. Here are some other possible sites of gallows or gibbets:

Gallows Knoll, Hopton

Gallows Yard, Taxal

Galley Acres field, Bakewell

Galleywood, or Three Shires, Bridge, near Flash

Gallowlow Lane, near Minninglow, High Peak Trail

Gautries Hill, Peak Forest; recorded as 'Gallow-trees' in 1617

Gibbet Moor, east of Chatsworth

Gib Hill, the Neolithic long barrow near Arbor Low

Gib Tor, Staffordshire Moorlands, the northernmost extension of
    Ramshaw Rocks

Dethick, near Matlock; literally meaning 'death oak'

Treak Cliff, Castleton; first recorded as 'Trayoc' in 1285, meaning
    'the oak of pain and suffering'

CHAPTER FIVE

Skulduggery

The Victorian engineers of the London and North Western Railway Company, in the nature of their breed, were not used to anything or anybody standing in their way. Their carefully-planned and costed route linking Buxton to Whaley Bridge and thence to Manchester had been surveyed to cross the deep Combs Valley on a high embankment, with a viaduct carrying the railway over the road.

The year was 1863, and it was at the height of a period of intense rivalry between the London and North Western and the Midland Railway Companies as they battled to be the first to complete the link to the spa town of Buxton, and capture the lucrative tourist trade which was expected to accrue, well ahead of their competitors.

The Midland had eventually overcome the many, apparently insurmountable problems which had been thrown at them, as they pushed their line from Rowsley through the Peak District hills. Competition had been equally hot between the major landowners – the Dukes of Devonshire at Chatsworth and Rutland at nearby Haddon. At first, the Duke of Rutland had been implacably opposed to the line going through his land in the Wye Valley, forcing the company to look at a route through Chatsworth Park and the valley of the River Derwent.

But that would have missed out Bakewell, and following pressure from townspeople and while the Duke of Devonshire prevaricated about the possible damage to his Capability Brown parkland, the Duke of Rutland was eventually persuaded to reconsider. He changed his mind, persuaded the House of Lords to turn down the Chatsworth proposal, and allowed a cut-and-cover tunnel to pass through the Haddon grounds. But this exercise had unfortunate consequences when the tunnel collapsed as it was under construction in July, 1861, killing five men.

The ducal duo were still at odds and both were anxious to see that the other did not have an advantage, a situation which was eventually resolved when it was agreed that Hassop station would become the Duke of Devonshire's stop for Chatsworth, while Bakewell station carried the Rutland coat of arms as the official station for Haddon Hall.

The controversy did not end there either, because the early conservationist John Ruskin chose the construction of the Midland line through Monsal Dale as the subject for one of his most fierce and famous outbursts against the rampant commercialisation of his age. Writing in *Fors Clavigera* in 1896, he fumed:

There was a rocky valley between Buxton and Bakewell, once upon a time as divine as the Vale of Tempe; you might have seen the Gods there morning and evening – Apollo and all the sweet Muses of the light – walking in fair procession on the lawns of it, and to and fro among the pinnacles of its crags. You cared neither for Gods nor grass, but for cash (which you did not know the way to get); you thought you could get it by what The Times calls "Railroad Enterprise". You Enterprised a Railroad through the valley – you blasted its rocks away, heaped thousands of tons of shale into its lovely stream. The valley is gone, and the Gods with it; and now, every fool in Buxton can be at Bakewell in half an hour, and every fool in Bakewell at Buxton; which you think a lucrative process of exchange – you Fools Everywhere.

Ironically, the viaduct which spans the Wye at Monsal Head is now an officially protected listed structure, and an accepted and much-loved part of one of the most-photographed views in the Peak.

The route chosen by the London and North Western Railway was a little less controversial, and was ultimately determined by its acquisition of the Stockport, Disley and Whaley Bridge, opened in 1857, which was extended to Buxton by way of Doveholes.

It was originally intended that the route should continue south through the Goyt Valley using the Cromford and High Peak Railway, but here the LNWR also ran into opposition from the local landowner – in this case Samuel Grimshawe of Errwood Hall, the Italianate mansion which overlooked the valley. He objected to the thought of a double-track, possible main line, passing through his moorland wilderness, even though a 4-mile tunnel under Long Hill would have been used to take the line into Buxton.

Eventually, the route left Whaley Bridge on a viaduct and climbed south-east up Randal Carr Brook, a tributary of the Goyt, under Ladder Hill and Combs Edge and into the Combs Valley.

But that is when Dickie objected.

We have already seen in Chapter Two that the worship of heads in the Peak District is an ancient and, in some places, still current, practice. But

The Monsal Head viaduct on the Midland Line – subject of John Ruskin's wrath.

perhaps the most famous and revered head of all is Dickie o'Tunstead, a disembodied skull which resided at Tunstead Farm, which is tucked under the escarpment of Ladder Hill and overlooks the Combs Reservoir.

Just who Dickie was is open to conjecture. Some people claim that 'he' was associated with a prehistoric burial at the now-lost nearby Cadster stone circle, and there are records of an Iron Age stone beehive quern being found on the farm. Chapel-en-le-Frith historian William Bunting claimed in 1940 that an examination of the skull by an eminent surgeon had concluded that they belonged to a young woman of around eighteen. He also suggested that the skull was found in one of the many prehistoric barrows, or 'lows', on the hillside above the farm, and had been taken into the house because of the local superstition which said that heads or skulls offered protection against evil spirits.

The most popular story however is that he was a Tunstead man called Ned Dickson, who fought in France during the Huguenot Wars of the sixteenth century. He distinguished himself at the Battle of Ivry, when on three separate occasions, he rescued Lord Willoughby after he had been unhorsed, in the process of which he was severely injured himself, lying out all night on the battlefield. Rescuers feared for his survival, but he eventually made an amazing recovery and returned to Derbyshire.

On his return home to Tunstead Farm, he found that his cousin, Jack Johnson, and his wife had given him up for dead, married, and claimed possession of the farm in his long absence. The disgruntled couple were obviously not best pleased to see Ned, but they invited him to spend the night at the farm. According to local tradition, they murdered him in his bed that night and secretly buried him on the farm, hoping no one would suspect what had happened.

But then things started to go wrong for the guilty couple, much as they had for Allan and Clara's murderers in the Winnats Pass. They were haunted by strange and unexplained noises, illness and the failure of their crops. The hauntings came to a head, as it were, when on a winter night less than a year after the murder, the dead man's head appeared to the terrified couple. The gruesome story was related by the nineteenth-century Derbyshire poet William Bennett:

> 'What's that i' the nook, John?' she suddenly cried,
> And shaking with terror they clearly espied
> The head of Ned Dickson upright on the stone,
> As wan and as ghastly as when he was done.

The years went by, and eventually the inevitable retribution struck the guilty couple down. She was killed when her husband hit her, and he died when an ancient oak tree growing on the farm inexplicably fell down on him.

The problem with this story is that investigation of the records show that no one called Dickson or Dixon owned the farm during the sixteenth century, and it is not mentioned in the earliest guidebooks. Perhaps it was the invention of the vivid imagination of William Bennett.

Another legend recounts that the skull was that of one of two co-heiresses to the farm who was brutally murdered and expressed as her dying wish that her bones should never be removed from the house. Certainly the legend is consistent that while Dickie is left where he is, he will protect the owners, but woe betide anyone who attempts to remove him.

There is the tale of one farmer being roused from his sleep by Dickie just as one of his prized cows was in danger of being strangled by its own chain, and on another occasion, a farmer and his wife were returning home from market in their cart, and the woman was facing the weary task of having to get down and open and close each gate as they passed through. 'I wish Dickie would open the gates,' she complained, whereupon to their astonishment, each gate opened as they approached it and conveniently closed behind them.

It is when the skull is removed that the trouble starts. Weird sounds, screams and disembodied voices haunt the house, and there is no rest for the occupants. It was once taken to be buried in Chapel churchyard, but the basket in which it was being carried got heavier and heavier as it was taken further away from the farm. On another occasion, it was thrown into Combs Reservoir, and all the fish in it mysteriously died, and while the farmhouse was being rebuilt, an unwise worker threw it carelessly into a manure heap. But the builders immediately found their work constantly being hampered, they heard screaming and unearthly moaning, and when they returned to work in the morning they found the previous day's work had been undone by the restless spirit. When the skull was restored inside the building, all was well again.

But Dickie's greatest triumph was to be at the expense of the great London and North Eastern Railway. At one stage, the development which was taking the line through the Combs Valley looked as if it would disturb Dickie's peace, and pass across the land belonging to Tunstead Farm. The farmer objected to no avail – then Dickie stepped in.

The embankment was built, and a bridge built to carry the road to the farm over the trackbed of the railway. Then things started to go wrong. The bridge sank into the marshy ground and its stonework was dislodged. The ground at each end of the arch was thrown up into huge mounds, and despite enormous and expensive efforts to rectify the situation, it was to no avail.

Of course, the logical explanation was that the embankment had been built on unstable ground – but local people preferred to think it was Dickie at work, protecting his home.

According to Dickie's 'biographer', William Bennett, writing in *The Reliquary*: 'The Railway Company and contractors battled with the malign power a long time, but they were eventually obliged to give way, and not only remove their bridge some distance, but form a new highway at a great expense for upwards of a quarter-of-a-mile.'

Contemporary local dialect poet Samuel Laycock expressed it thus:

> *Neaw, Dickie, be quiet wi' thee, lad,*
> *An' let the navvies an' railways a' be;*
> *Mon than shouldn't do soa, its too bad,*
> *What harm are they doin' to thee?*
> *Deed folk shouldn't meddle at o',*
> *But leov o' these matters to th' wick;*
> *They'll see they're done gradely, aw know –*
> *Dos' t' yer what aw say to thee, Dick?*

But Dickie wasn't listening, and a new and expensive road and bridge eventually had to be constructed into the Combs Valley, well away from the farm and its marshy entrance.

Dickie is by no means the only skull which acts as a good luck charm in some older Peak District houses. Another was traditionally kept on a window sill at Dunscar Farm, on the slopes running up to Mam Tor near Castleton, and yet another is well-documented high on the White Peak plateau at Flagg Hall, even being accepted as part of the house's valuation.

The same tradition exists of tales of misfortune should the skull be removed or abused in any way. It was once taken to be given a decent Christian burial at nearby Chelmorton churchyard, but on reaching a point known as Chelmorton Thorn, the horses drawing the makeshift hearse stamped their hooves, reared up and refused to go further. No amount of inducement would make them move forward, and eventually, they were turned around and the skull was returned to its accustomed place in a glass case at Flagg Hall.

A similar story tells of a servant girl who got fed up with the grisly sight of the skull and impetuously threw it out of the window. It landed on top of a manure cart being drawn by a horse, which promptly once again refused to move further until the skull was returned inside the house.

Was Dickie really responsible for holding up the mighty LNER, and were those other tales of restless skulls just old wives' tales? Perhaps it's just a case of 'tales' they win, and heads you lose...

☙❧

THE QUIET WOMAN

The Quiet Woman is the name of the village public house at Earl Sterndale, above the Upper Dove Valley. The inn sign shows the body of a headless woman, dressed in flowing Tudor costume and her hands in a muff, with the ironic inscription beneath: 'Soft Words Turneth Away Wrath.' The story is that this is a depiction of 'Chattering Charteris', the wife of a former landlord, whose constant chattering and nagging eventually drove her desperate husband to behead her.

CHAPTER SIX
A Plague on all your Houses

Ring- a-ring o' roses
A pocket full o' posies
Atishoo! Atishoo!
We all fall down

The children dancing round hand-in-hand in a ring in the playground of St Lawrence's Church of England Primary School in Eyam were using a nursery rhyme which, like many of their kind, had been passed down for generations from child to child.

But how many of them knew that the playground game and rhyme they were chanting was in fact a pretty accurate summary of the symptoms and deadly results of the plague which had famously decimated their hillside village 340 years ago? Perhaps because the imagined scene was in Eyam, where nearly three and a half centuries on the story of the plague is still an ever-present background to everyday life, they did realise the significance of their game.

Although they are usually unaware of the fact, children are often among the most important preservers of our traditions and folklore. The games they play and the rhymes they chant in the playground are often very old, and passed on not by adults but by succeeding generations of children. Some of the words they use are very ancient, such as the truce words of 'barley' – as used in the north-west of England, which appears in works dating as far back as the fourteenth century; and 'pax', which is more universal and comes of course from the Latin.

To return to the Eyam playground and explain the symptomatic nature of the rhyme; the 'ring o' roses' is the purple rash or 'macula' which appeared on the chest of a doomed plague victim. The 'pocket full of posies' relates to the pomanders or nosegays of sweet-smelling herbs and spices which were carried by women because they were thought to prevent the inhalation of the plague spores, when it was believed that they were spread by poisonous odours or fumes known as 'miasma'.

The sneezing represented the symptoms which resembled the onset of a chill: shivering and headaches and the sneezing, which actually was the major cause of the spread of the disease in the expelled droplets. Finally, 'We all fall down' is the chilling and, in the seventeenth century, inescapable fate of a victim – a painful and lingering death.

The story of the self-imposed quarantine of the village of Eyam during the terrible 'visitation' of the plague in the fateful years of 1665-66 has been described as 'an epic in the annals of rural life', and the public's seemingly-never ending fascination with it attracts thousands of tourists every year.

When the plague struck the villagers, led by their young rector, William Mompesson and his much-loved nonconformist predecessor, Thomas Stanley, nobly resolved to impose a *cordon sanitaire* around the village to prevent the spread of the dread disease to other parts of the county.

Estimates vary quite widely in the mortality rate suffered by the brave villagers, with some commentators and modern guidebooks still putting the rate as high as five-sixths of the population – 259 people out of a population of 350. The truth is that the population of the parish of Eyam at this time was between 850 and 1000 – so the mortality rate was still probably between a quarter and a third. This is still comparatively high compared with the estimated 17 per cent death rate from the plague in London in 1665-66, when between 70,000 and 100,000 people died.

Some modern commentators have been critical of the villagers' decision to stay put to try to contain the outbreak. They claim that their policy of containment probably made matters much worse than it needed to have been – giving the rural outbreak of the disease a mortality rate more like that of a severe outbreak in a city or town. One authority has gone so far as to say that the plague of Eyam was 'a disaster that need not have happened.'

The most natural instinct in circumstances such as these would be to pack up and leave, and this is exactly what most of the wealthier inhabitants of the village, including the Sheldon family and the Mompessons did with their children. But in fact this was simply not possible for the poorer residents, the farmers, miners and labourers. They could not just abandon their livelihoods, and in any case, where could they go?

As soon as the news escaped that the plague had struck in Eyam, other neighbouring villages worried by the threat of infection made it perfectly clear that refugees from Eyam would not be welcome. The people of Sheffield even erected barriers at entrances to their town and manned guard posts to prevent possibly-infected strangers from entering. There is a well documented case of a fugitive from Orchard Bank who tried to flee to Tideswell but was stopped by a 'border guard'. When questioned, she said

This is where the plague began. The Plague Cottages, Eyam.

she was from 'the land of the living' and allowed to pass. But it was market day in 'Tidser', and she was soon recognised and summarily evicted by an angry crowd.

So in reality, the poorer villagers did not have much choice but to stay put and face the awful consequences of the plague.

The tradition is that the infection arrived in Eyam in September, 1665, via a box of cloth from plague-hit London, although some accounts put its place of origin as Canterbury. When the tercentenary of the 'visitation' was celebrated in Eyam in 1965, the programme even included an apology from Sir James Miller, Lord Mayor of London, because, he said, history implied that the disease had been 'passed to Eyam from this old city.' He sent the capital's very best wishes for the next three hundred years.

George Viccars, a journeyman tailor, was a lodger at the gritstone cottage home of Mary Cooper, adjacent to the churchyard. The clothing in his box may have been secondhand, but in any case, when the box was opened the contents were found to be damp, so they were laid out in front of the fire to dry. Shortly after this, Viccars became ill and within a week, he was dead – the first victim of the Eyam plague.

49

The plague bacilli is spread by fleas which live on the house or black rat (*Rattus rattus*), which was rife in London during the mid-seventeenth century. Usually found now in ports or docklands, it has been claimed that neither it nor its fleas could have survived the bleak Peakland winters as experienced in Eyam.

It is thought that the cloth brought by Viccars contained black rat fleas or their eggs, infected by the plague bacilli. The fleas would normally feed on the blood of their rat hosts, but finding none in Eyam, they would have taken the next available alternative, the unfortunate Viccars.

Having claimed its first victim, the disease took about a fortnight to establish itself in the village and the next victim was Edward Cooper, one of Mary Cooper's sons. In total, there were six deaths in the space of three weeks, with all the victims coming from neighbouring cottages.

It is not difficult to imagine the hysteria and panic which must have spread through the close-knit community of Eyam, where like today, everyone knew everyone else. By the end of October, 29 people had died, exceeding the average annual death rate of the previous decade. People knew that the plague was always most virulent in the warmer summer months, so they must have viewed the approach of winter with some relief. But the end of winter, i.e. April 1666, there had already been 73 deaths, most of which it is thought were due to the plague.

It was then that the rector, only twenty-eight years of age and recently arrived in the parish in 1664, decided to work together with Thomas Stanley, his dispossessed staunchly Puritan predecessor. They resolved to set aside their obvious religious differences for the greater good. It is well attested that Stanley was respected and liked in the village, and in the last analysis, it was probably only the tragic circumstances which threw them together which ensured the ultimate success of their brave decision.

After an initial meeting held at the rectory, the two ministers came up with the courageous idea of quarantining the village in order to halt the spread of the awful disease to surrounding communities. They still had to sell the idea to the villagers themselves, but the presenting of a united moral and religious front must have been a major influence to induce many villagers to accept the plan.

The interdenominational plan required three major decisions:
– no more organised funerals or burials. People were advised to bury their dead in their gardens or in the fields, in an attempt to halt the spread of infection.
– The church should be locked until the epidemic had passed, and services

The Saxon cross in Eyam churchyard.

51

would be held in the open air. Cucklet Delph, a natural limestone amphitheatre in the dale below the village, was used for these open air services.

– The cordon sanitaire would be imposed around the village boundary to halt the spread of infection to the outside world.

These were all tough decisions which must have resulted in much heart-searching and anguish for the villagers of Eyam. They must have known, and perhaps Mompesson and Stanley even told them, that they were in effect sentencing many of their number to a certain, painful death. But such was the strength of their Christian faith, they resolved to try to keep the dread disease within their boundaries.

Even in those days, a small village like Eyam could not be wholly self-sufficient. They would need supplies, particularly food, from outside if their bold and selfless plan was to succeed. That was when the major local landowner, William Cavendish, the 4th Earl (later to become the 1st Duke) of Devonshire of Chatsworth became the chief benefactor. He arranged for food and medical supplies to be left near the Boundary Stone on the southern edge of the village.

Cynics have said that this was a small price to pay for his own protection, and that in the hour of their greatest need, the poorest villagers of Eyam were probably fed better at the Earl's expense than at any previous time in their lives.

Other supplies were left by neighbouring villagers at the site now known as Mompesson's Well on the slopes of Sir William Hill above Eyam Edge overlooking the village, and at the remote Bronze Age stone circle of Wet Withins on heather-clad Eyam Moor, further to the north. Then as now, the local market was held at Bakewell on a Monday, and it was during the plague period that the stream near Stockingcote became known as Mondaybrook, as the villagers made their purchases from the market through others safely across the stream.

To ensure the infection would not spread, the Eyam villagers left their payment for the supplies either in running water, as at the well or in Mondaybrook, or in vinegar-filled holes in convenient rocks, such as can still be seen in the Boundary Stone to the south of the village.

Many cottages in the village today carry plaques which record the names of those who died there during those dreadful days of the visitation of the plague in Eyam. There were many heart-rending and tragic stories associated with this terrible period, but perhaps none are as poignant as those of the neighbouring Talbot and Hancock families, who lived a mile from the village on the road to Grindleford.

All 12 members of the Talbot family died from the plague during July 1666, from old Bridget Talbot, widow of a former rector, to her great grandchild, three-month-old Catherine. Then the pestilence spread to their friends and neighbours, the Hancocks.

Within ten terrible days, eight members of the family died, and Mrs Hancock was faced with the gruesome task of burying her husband and seven of her children, one by one, in the fields around her home, watched by the villagers of Stoney Middleton in the valley below. Not surprisingly, it all proved too much for her, and she left the village to live with her only remaining son, who was an apprentice cutler in Sheffield.

For many people, the so-called Riley Graves, which take their name from their locality at Top Riley and which are the collected gravestones of the Hancock family, are the most touching reminders of the plague years in Eyam. Isolated and now badly-weathered, they stand in a circular drystone wall enclosure on the old Grindleford road, and are now in the care of the National Trust. Scattered around the village out in the fields can be found many other simple gravestones where families hastily buried their dead in unconsecrated ground.

The only known plague grave in the churchyard of St Lawrence's at Eyam is the table-top tomb of Catherine Mompesson, the wife of the rector, who died in August, 1666. They had been out for a walk when, to her husband's dismay, she remarked: 'Oh Mompesson, the air! How sweet it smells!' He knew that one of the first symptoms of the plague was a sickly-sweet sensation in the nostrils. Mompesson's letter informing his children of their mother's loss is one of the most moving and pathetic documents to survive the plague years.

Eventually, fourteen long months after it had begun, the plague finally released its grisly hold on Eyam. It had claimed the lives of around 260 of the residents, but the courageous master plan of Mompesson and Stanley had worked, and the infection had not spread to the rest of the county.

But was it really the plague which was responsible for the horrific death toll at Eyam? Some learned academics have questioned the fact, claiming that during those times, any rampantly-infectious disease was automatically called a 'plague', and it could just as easily have been typhus, anthrax – or even the measles.

The lack of any records of dead or dying livestock seems to rule out anthrax, but there are similarities between the initial stages of typhus and measles. The excellent Eyam Museum in Hawkhill Road lists no less than 33 symptoms for the plague as recorded by seventeenth-century doctors.

And what of the survivors? Some villagers, notably the sexton Marshall Howe who was responsible for burying many of the victims, seemed to be immune from the disease and survived the 'visitation' along with the majority of the other villagers.

Recent research in America has thrown new light on this phenomenon. Geneticists have isolated a rare hereditary gene called Delta 32, which prevents the destruction of body cells by the plague bacilli. The still relatively static population of Eyam encouraged them to come to the village in 2002 to give DNA tests to known descendants of plague survivors.

The results showed that there was a far higher incidence of the Delta 32 gene in these people than had been found anywhere else. And an intriguing bonus is that this same mutant gene may also offer protection from the modern day plague which is sweeping the world – the AIDS virus.

⨂

THE CURBAR PLAGUE

How many of the thousands who visit Eyam each year to hear the heroic story of the 'visitation' of the plague realise that the neighbouring village of Curbar, just 4 miles away, suffered a similar fate thirty-three years before? The Plague of Curbar is not so well chronicled, but the discovery of several roughly-hewn slabs on the edge of the moors beneath the crags of Curbar Edge proved that it was just as harrowing.

The first of the stones to be discovered were a group of five inscribed: T.C. 1632, A.C., O.C., N.C. and T.C. are thought to be the memorials of Thomas Cundy, his wife, Ada, and their three children, Olive, Nellie and Thomas who lived nearby at Grislowfields Farm. Tradition stated that other families – including the Sheldons, Cookes or Clarkes – were plague victims at the time, and buried in an orchard at the bottom end of the village. This was confirmed by the discovery of a slab inscribed I. or J.C. 1632 there in 1967, and yet another 200 yards from the Cundy graves in 1975, inscribed H.W. 1632. In both these cases, the '3' was carved in reverse, probably indicating the work of the same semi-literate local craftsman.

CHAPTER SEVEN

Stemples of Doom

One for sorrow, two for joy,
Three for a girl and four for a boy,
Five for silver, six for gold,
Seven for a secret never to be told.

Another rhyme learned in the playground about counting magpies starts this chapter, but the 'secret never to be told' in this case relates to a tale of murder and mystery which took place 170 years ago, 420 feet (128m) below the surface of the rolling White Peak plateau.

Magpie Mine, near Sheldon, is the most complete and evocative remains of an eighteenth- and nineteenth-century lead mine in the Peak District, and probably in the whole of Britain. It has been worked off and on for 300 years, and the stark remains of the engine house and twin chimneys are prominent landmarks on the back road between Bakewell and Chelmorton.

A solitary visit to the surface remains at Magpie is always imbued with an air of mystery and some would say, menace. As you walk over the cattle grids and up the trackway which leads to the Victorian (1840) Agent's House and Smithy, which now provides a field centre for the Peak District Mines Historical Society, the remaining mine buildings and their associated memories begin to crowd in on you. And in the back of your mind, you know that a widow's curse still hangs over these now-deserted buildings.

To the left beyond the Smithy stands the square chimney built in 1840 by John Taylor on the site of the old Winding House, it is said, by Derbyshire miners who never quite mastered the art of building circular structures. Ahead rises the gaunt black-painted steel Winding Wheel, which stands astride the awesome 728 feet (222m) deep Main Shaft. The adjacent black corrugated iron shed housed a winch during the last, futile attempt to win ore from the mine by what was orginally a New Zealand company in 1951. The loose sheets which now clang spookily in the wind are part of what is now one of the youngest protected structures in the National Park.

Behind is the massive, church-like engine house, built in 1869 by John Fairburn, which contained an enormous 12 feet (3.6m) high and 70in-

Skeletal trees frame the haunted remains of Magpie Mine, near Sheldon.

diameter cylinder, and alongside is the stately circular Cornish chimney, originally built in 1840. The round structure in the fields behind is the powder house where explosives were stored, and is another designed by the 20 or so Cornish miners who came to Magpie in 1839 when the mine was re-opened by John Taylor.

The biggest problem faced by lead miners in the Peak District was water, and they knew that huge reserves of lead ore were being barred to them because of the high water levels which existed in the mines. When John Fairburn took over Magpie in 1864, he ran into the same problem, and brought in that huge pump engine from Calver Sough Mine which initially was successful in draining the shaft. But he knew that greater reserves lay deeper, so in 1873 he started the construction of the famous mile-long Magpie Sough, which would empty the water into the River Wye west of Ashford-in-the-Water. A sough (pronounced 'suff') is an adit driven through the rocks specifically to drain a mine.

Eight years and at least £18,000 later, Fairburn organised a dinner for his workmen to celebrate the opening of the sough, and the 'de-watering' of the mine. Two years later, however, mining operations had ceased, John Fairburn was declared bankrupt and he died a broken man shortly afterwards.

The spoil heaps which surround the buildings at Magpie Mine are obviously heavily impregnated with traces of the highly poisonous lead ore, or galena, which you would think would be anathema to any kind of flowering plant. Not so, and if you come to Magpie in early summer you will find these unpromising banks ablaze with wild flowers – another of Magpie's mysteries.

A clue is the fact that the abundant, snowy-white cushions of spring sandwort are known locally as 'leadwort', because the miners knew that this delicate little alpine shows an extremely high tolerance of lead pollution. The same applies to alpine penny cress – also sometimes known as leadwort – bird's foot trefoil (also known as 'bacon and eggs'), maiden pink, dark mullein and a range of early purple orchids.

But perhaps the finest display on Magpie's mine-tips is that of the mountain pansies, which here, on the banks of the old slime ponds and dressing floors, show every variation of colour, from pure purple and yellow to hybrids with petals of both colours.

Over the flower-strewn humps and hollows of former workings to the east of the main buildings can be seen the wooden framework of the restored horse gin (horse-powered winding engine), which stands over the deep shaft of the Great Redsoil Mine. This marks the site, 400 feet underground, of the infamous 'murders on the mine' in 1833.

This view of Magpie Mine is from the reconstructed horse gin over the Redsoil shaft, scene of the 1833 dispute.

Magpie Mine had been worked since 1740, and since then, various veins of ore had been discovered criss-crossing under the pastures around the site. There were often disputes over ownership of these veins, usually resolved by reference to the local Barmote Courts, which constituted some of the oldest surviving courts in the country.

But the troubles at Magpie began in earnest in September, 1824, when miners from the Maypitt Mine – later known as the Redsoil Mine – broke through into Magpie Mine workings on the Bole Vein. From May, 1825, an almost constant stream of bills and cross bills claiming ownership were filed to the Barmote Court, and decisions went either way.

These legal actions culminated in August, 1833, when both Magpie and Redsoil miners were employed to guard their possessions, and men were even 'tented', or camped out underground, to ensure that the other side did not attempt to take the vein.

On August 30, following an incident when the Redsoil men had refused to allow the Magpie men access for blasting, an explosion in the Magpie workings injured a Redsoil man. In retaliation, Redsoil lit a fire of straw to try to 'smoke out' the Magpie men, and prevent them from removing the Redsoil 'gates' – the name given to an access route in a mine.

The Magpie miners produced a counter fire the following day and, as they

59

had intended, the smoke drifted through to the Redsoil workings, causing one man to collapse. It was alleged that the Magpie miners had lowered a bottle of gas oil into the engine shaft. According to a contemporary account, smoke poured out of the shafts 'like Manchester factory chimneys.'

These actions rendered the Redsoil mine virtually unworkable for the next few days, and allowed the Magpie men the access they required. The Redsoil agent, Henry Knowles, ordered the smoking shafts to be covered, in an attempt to drive the smoke back into the Magpie workings.

Then on September 2, two Redsoil miners named Wildgoose and Mottram, descended the Redsoil shaft to check the workings. When they returned, although Mottram collapsed from the fumes and they also said the mine was unfit to work in, they reported that the smoke was not as thick below 20 fathoms (120ft/36m).

So other men were sent below by Knowles to prevent the Magpie miners from removing their access. But the smoke was thicker than expected, and many of the men when they tried to return found they could not retrace their steps back to the surface, and they became overcome by the choking fumes of smoke. Two miners called Heathcote and Ashton, struggled to the surface and reported that unless rescuers arrived immediately, their colleagues trapped below would perish.

Fellow miners and their wives rushed to the scene and began to pour water down the smoking shaft in an attempt to quench the fires. Eventually, when rescuers eventually arrived, the lifeless bodies of Issac Bagshawe, Francis Taylor and Thomas Wager were retrieved from the bottom of the shaft.

At the trial held at Derby Assizes six months later, 24 miners from Magpie were arraigned before the court, although the majority were immediately set free. Ten miners were charged with 'feloniously, wilfully and maliciously' murdering Taylor, Bagshawe and Wager, 'by means of noxious and unwholesome drugs and poisons which impregnated the air where the deceased men were working.'

They were represented by a wily lawyer, William Brittlebank of Winster – once rather sarcastically described as 'not the only knave in Derbyshire' – who produced a written defence which was read out in court, since at the time the accused were not allowed to speak in their own defence.

This suggested to some observers at least that the action which had caused the death of the three Redsoil miners was conducted in self-defence, and that the Redsoil agent, knowing it was permissable to use fires in the mine, had sent his men down the shaft in the full knowledge that it was dangerously full of smoke.

The judge, Justice Littledale, said he was dubious of the murder charge,

Magpie Mine, near Sheldon – scene of underground murders.

as the Redsoil miners' evidence showed that they were equally responsible for underground fires, and had contributed to their own demise by shutting off the shafts. In his four-hour summing-up, he also instructed the jury that there was doubt over whether the Magpie miners had intended to injure deliberately 'beyond that of annoyance.'

Whatever the reasons, the ten miners were acquitted.

But local legend states that the widow of one of the dead miners raised a curse over the Magpie Mine – a curse which saw a series of mysterious accidents and all subsequent attempts to re-open the mine and make a profit from the precious ore which is known to exist underground end in disaster. And many people believe it is a curse which stands even until today.

The limestone area around Castleton at the head of the Hope Valley was famously described by Sir Arthur Conan Doyle, creator of the most famous detective in English literature.

All this country is hollow. Could you strike it with some gigantic hammer it would boom like a drum, or possibly cave in altogether and expose some huge subterranean sea. A great sea there must surely be, for on all sides the streams run into the mountain itself, never to reappear. There are gaps everywhere amid the rocks, and when you pass through them you find yourself in great caverns, which wind down into the bowels of the earth.

This description is taken from Conan Doyle's short story, *The Terror of Blue John Gap*, in which a curious recuperating TB sufferer staying on a farm near Castleton ventures into a Roman Blue John mine with a sinister reputation.

Dr James Hardcastle eventually meets up with the terrifying bear-like creature which is apparently responsible for the deaths of many local sheep, and the source of blood-curdling sounds which periodically emanate from the cave. One dark and moonless night, he lays in wait for the creature and shoots it, following the wounded creature deep into the cave, where it turns and attacks him. He is recovered unconscious from the cave and the sinister slot is finally sealed by villagers.

The doctor's theory is that the beast was a blind denizen of that subterranean world of plants and animals which he believed existed under the limestone, and which had somehow escaped into the open air.

Perhaps Conan Doyle based his 'Tale of Terror' on stories he had heard while staying near Castleton, because a very similar malediction seems to linger around the evil gash of the Odin Mine, beneath the 'Shivering

Mountain' of Mam Tor. First recorded in 1208, this is said to be the oldest lead mine in the Peak.

The story here is that it is haunted by the ghost of one of the Winnats Pass murderers of Allan and Clara (see Chapter 4), and another persistent local legend claims that no less than 70 lead miners were drowned when the mine was flooded after a sudden event of 'slickensides' – the violent explosion of splintering rock which can occur when there is a build up of pressure along a geological fault.

Perhaps it is the evil reputation of Odin Mine (named, incidentally, after the Norse god of death, wisdom, magic and madness), but it also has a bad reputation among local cavers and is described in their guidebook as 'unstable and potentially dangerous.' So when I was invited to join a local club for an excursion down Odin a few years ago, it was with some trepidation, as a novice caver, that I finally accepted. I was soon to discover that all those dire warnings were perfectly justified, and it remains one of the most uncomfortable and frightening experiences of my life.

To get to the entrance, we had to clamber up past evidence of the pick marks made in the walls by the early miners, to a very greasy fallen ash tree at the back of the gorge. I subconsciously wondered if it was Odin's fabled ash, Yggdrasill, leading to the entrance to the underworld.

Two narrow slits led underground, and an equally-greasy 10 feet (3m) of fixed rope gave access to the Little Shaft Vein, which I entered with a slither and landed with a splash in a foot of muddy water. We walked down the worked-out vein, passing 'cross-cuts' (passages cut from one vein to another), 'sumps' (internal shafts), and 'scrins' (thin, vertical veins of ore). Having got this far, I decided it was a case of scrin and bear it.

Passing around a seemingly bottomless water-filled hole on a fixed rope, we entered a passage, ducking underneath crumbling wooden 'stemples' – overhead beams on which waste materials, ominously known as 'deads', were stacked. Eventually and much to my relief, the precarious wooden stemples gave way to more robust ones of beautifully-dressed stone.

Then we reached the notorious 35-foot (10m) pitch, descended by means of a tiny aluminium ladder which I embraced with a passion born of sheer adrenalin ... and naked fear. Another short descent led to our final objective – the Cartgate Chamber, a soaring, 60-foot (18m) high underground cathedral capped with beautifully-crafted pitched roof. We marvelled at the skilled workmanship of 't'owd man', as the old miners are known, whose only illumination as they worked was a flickering candle stuffed on the brim of their 'Bradder' hats.

The author thankfully emerges from Odin Mine. (By courtesy of Fay Hartley)

A relieved author after his Odin Mine experience. (By courtesy of Fay Hartley)

The less said about my undignified exit from the mine, the better. Suffice to say that I was totally exhausted and had to be hauled up the 35-foot pitch to be landed like a muddy orange fish at the top. After about four hours underground, we eventually emerged under that fateful fallen ash and into what passes for daylight in a late February afternoon at Castleton.

To say I was relieved would be an understatement. But I certainly now had first-hand experience of the curse of Odin... and this particular Indiana Jones won't be going back into that 'Stemple of Doom' in a hurry.

'T'OWD MAN' TERMINOLOGY

The language of the old lead miners of the White Peak is as colour-ful as it is ancient. The following are a few of their terms, some of which are still in use today:

Barmote – the miners' court, usually held twice a year, with a 12-man jury.

Bole – a common placename usually on a hill top, which indicates the site of a lead smelting hearth.

Cross-cut – passage cut from one vein to another.

Deads – waste stone from a vein or working.

Nicking – if a mine was not being worked, another could make a 'nick' in the wooden windlass over the mine. After three nicks, the mine would be forfeited to the new owner. Even today, 'nicking' still means stealing something from another.

Rake – a large vein of ore, often running for miles across country and marked by rows of trees, planted to stop cattle from entering.

Scrin – a thin, vertical vein of ore, often branching out of a rake.

Slickensides – shiny, grooved surfaces produced by movement along geological faults which can sometimes explode under stress.

Sough – an adit or tunnel driven through the limestone to drain water from a mine.

Stemple – a wooden wedge across a working, sometimes used as a roof support or platform for stacking 'deads'.

CHAPTER EIGHT

Ghost Villages

Sheep have eaten up our meadows and our downs
Our corn, our wood, whole villages and towns.
Yea, they have eat up many wealthy men
Besides widows and orphan children:
 – Thomas Bastard, *Epigrams*, 1598

It's a strange fact, but places where people have lived, loved and laughed in the past always seem to be more lonely when deserted than places where people have never settled.

Examples can be found in many of the upland areas of Britain: in the many abandoned sheilings of the western Scottish Highlands and islands, where greedy and uncaring landlords evicted huge numbers of their tenants to replace them with more profitable sheep in the eighteenth and nineteenth centuries; in the west of Ireland where the 'Great Hunger' caused by the potato famine of the 1840s saw hundreds of thousands of farmworkers and their families forced to emigrate to the USA and Canada; and also in the abandoned grey slate villages of Snowdonia.

They always seem to me to be more desolate and empty than the mountain wildernesses which surround them. An air of melancholy and sadness seems to hang around the ruined walls and gable ends, permeating into the skin and bones of the discerning visitor every bit as effectively as the weeping mists and rain which so often envelop them.

I get the same chilling feeling creeping up my spine when I take one of my favourite local walks across Haddon Fields, near my home in Bakewell. The humps and hollows which in the right light can be seen from the A6 in the rising fields opposite Haddon Hall mark the site of one of the Peak's several deserted medieval villages – collectively known to archaeologists as DMVs.

The desertion and disappearance of the former village of Nether Haddon follows a similar pattern to many which were deemed unprofitable and therefore expendable to the feudal manorial landlords of the Middle Ages. Many people know the ridgetop village of Over Haddon overlooking the

National Nature Reserve of Lathkill Dale, but far fewer know that at the time of the Domesday Book in 1086, there were two Haddons belonging to the royal manor of Bakewell. Nether – or 'Lower' – Haddon lay to the east of Over Haddon in the open fields which slope down towards the River Wye and Haddon Hall. In fact, in the first half of the fourteenth century, taxation returns show that Nether Haddon was by far the more important of the two settlements. In 1334 it was valued at 46 shillings and 2 pence while Over Haddon was only valued at 18 shillings and 2 pence.

At the time of Domesday, it had been recorded that Henry of Ferrers claimed one carucate (a unit of land as recorded in former Danish areas, equivalent to a hide or about 120 acres) which included the outlying settlements of Nether and Upper Haddon, Holme, Rowsley, Conkesbury, One Ash, Monyash and Burton.

The mention of Burton is interesting, because this is yet another lost settlement between Bakewell and Haddon. Recent research by local historian Jan Stetka has indicated that it may have taken its name from the burh or temporary fort erected by Edward the Elder in the Wye Valley near Bakewell in AD920, where he was apparently accepted as 'father and lord' by most of the kingships of Britain.

The lords of the manor of Nether Haddon in the fourteenth century were the powerful Vernon family of Haddon Hall, and it was during the tenure of Sir Richard Vernon IV that the fate of the village seems to have been sealed. In 1330, Richard, made wealthy from the income from the many local lead mines his family owned, was granted a licence to enclose a park. A few years later he completed a major rebuilding of the hall, including the central banqueting hall, kitchens and parlour we can still see today in this most complete of English medieval manor houses. His successor Richard VI also greatly enlarged the chapel in 1426, which at the time also served as the parish church of Nether Haddon, to create the present family chapel of St Nicholas, with its magnificent medieval wall-paintings.

While we cannot be precisely sure of the actual date of the desertion of Nether Haddon, it appears most likely that it coincided with the creation of a park around the hall in the years between 1350 and 1426. Certainly by 1431 the records show that Richard Vernon V was the sole tenant at Haddon, and therefore the village must have been depopulated.

The holloways of the former roads and low platforms and banks which define former yards and buildings are all that's left of Nether Haddon today. That and the surrounding corrugations left by ridge and furrow culti-

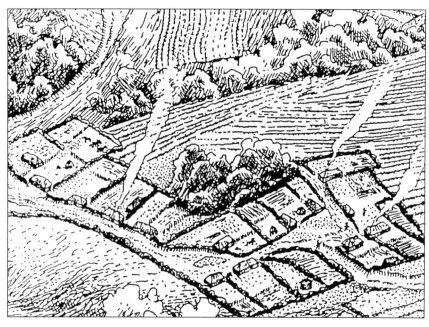

A reconstruction by John Barnatt of how Nether Haddon may have looked in medieval times. (By courtesy Dr John Barnatt)

What is left of the original Edensor village. The cottage known as Naboth's Vineyard in Chatsworth Park.

Inside the chapel – formerly the church of Nether Haddon – at Haddon Hall. (By courtesy Haddon Hall Estate)

vation of the former open fields, and the series of giant staircases of strip lynchets where cultivation took place on the steeper, sloping ground to the south. The walls of the buildings in which the residents of Nether Haddon lived were constructed of wattle and daub, and once the heather-thatched roof had gone, they were exposed to the harsh elements of a Peakland winter, and soon melted away into the rolling landscape as if they had never existed.

The sad story of Nether Haddon is echoed in many other places on the White Peak plateau, such as Balidon, Blackwell, Conksbury, Gratton, Smerril and Lea Hall, where often the only clue to a village's former existence is provided by aerial photography. All that exists at Balidon, in the dry valley which leads up to the Romano-British site of Roystone Grange and the massive limestone quarry, is the simple little locked Norman chapel, which stands all alone in a field, and a few scattered farmhouses.

Just across the hill from Haddon Hall and the former village of Nether Haddon is Chatsworth, the grand estate of the Dukes of Devonshire popularly known as 'the Palace of the Peak'. Successive Earls and Dukes of Devonshire have since the early seventeenth century remodelled and reshaped the contours of the Derwent Valley to suit their contemporary tastes in scenery. This has included the deliberate depopulation and replacement of at least three villages which formerly stood in Laurence 'Capability' Brown's rolling parkland.

The Domesday Book records no less than three settlements in the valley where the house now stands – Edensoure, Chetesourde and Langeleie – which were worth 20 shillings in the time of Edward the Confessor and only 16 shillings in 1086. Langley seems to have been last recorded in 1355, while the village of Chatsworth is still shown on the eastern bank of the Derwent on Christopher Saxton's map of 1577. It seems to have been a victim of the 4th Duke's comprehensive rebuilding of the house and extension of the park at the turn of the seventeenth century.

Edensor (pronounced 'Ensor'), of course, still exists as the neat little estate village across the Derwent from the Big House, but it was moved from its previous position between the river and the road and totally rebuilt by the 6th Duke and Joseph Paxton between 1838 and 1842. The legend is that the reason for the transplanting of Edensor was that it spoiled the view from the house, and that the one remaining cottage, sometimes known as Naboth's Vineyard, which was spared, still enclosed by its high, deer-proof walled garden, was the home of Thomas Holmes, an old and honoured retainer whom the Duke did not want to disturb.

One of the most chilling Latin phrases which constantly crops up in a reading of the Derbyshire chapters of the Domesday Book is *wasta est* – meaning 'it is waste'. Almost 50 manors in the Peak District are written off in this way, and most parishes, as with Chatsworth, Edensor and Langley quoted above, are worth considerably less in the years following the Norman Conquest than they were under the Saxon rule of Edward the Confessor.

Many historical commentators have attributed these stark facts to what has been described as the most fearful acts of genocide in English history, and have compared it with the ethnic cleansing undertaken by Adolf Hitler against the Jews during the Third Reich, or more recently by Nicolae Ceausescu in Romania.

The laying waste of large areas of the north of England from 1069-71 is somewhat innocently known as the Harrying of the North, and although it is said to have resulted in the deaths of 100,000 people, it usually gets scant mention in school history books. We have a first-hand account of the terrors of those years from the chronicler Orderic Vitalis, who travelled with William I's Norman storm troopers.

During this awful time, it is said that 100,000 people perished. It was terrible to see rotting corpses covered in multitudes of worms in the silent dwellings and deserted streets and roads with the atmosphere made foul by the stench of putrifaction. Nobody remained to bury the corpses... Nothing moved in the scorched ruins of villages but the packs of wolves and wild dogs which tore apart the human corpses.

The Harrying of the North took place after the murder of two Norman earls as they attempted to enter their recently-granted Northumbrian estates. William hastily sent his forces north to relieve and fortify his northern stronghold at York. Despite promises of Scottish and Danish support, the northern rebels were finally left to face the cruel Norman reprisals on their own, and William was typically ruthless.

The settlements laid waste in the Peak appear to be concentrated in the Upper Dove Valley from Ashbourne and Axe Edge northwards; in the Pennine foothills of East Cheshire, and throughout the whole of Longdendale, north of Bleaklow. More than 30 manors in East Cheshire were affected, while the Domesday entry for Longdendale simply states: 'All Longdendale is waste; woodland, unpastured, fit for hunting.' The value of this 72 square-mile area before 1066 had been 40 shillings, and now it was a worthless waste. Later, because that was all it was worth, it became part of the 40 square-mile Royal Forest of the Peak – a hunting ground set aside for

Birchinlee village, looking south down the Derwent Valley. (By courtesy of Prof. Brian Robinson)

the king and his cronies and administered from Peveril Castle at Castleton.

Not all Peak District townships were created and deserted in medieval times. Others have been founded, briefly thrived and then disappeared within living memory, and the most famous of these is the navvy village in the Upper Derwent Valley which was locally nicknamed Tin Town.

When the Derwent Valley Water Board resolved to build two dams to impound the water of the Derwent in the early years of the twentieth century to provide good clean water for the fast expanding cities of Sheffield and the East Midlands, it also decided that it should also provide decent accommodation for the 'navvies' who would build them.

The workmen's village of Birchinlee would be a model of its kind. Laid out along two roads which were pitched with stone, kerbed and provided with paraffin-burning street lights, the village was, as far as possible in such an isolated spot, self-sufficient.

It was served by the railway which brought the stone to the site from Grindleford, and had its own school, shops, public house or canteen, hospital, recreation hall and police station. As surviving photographs show, the workmen's huts were surprisingly luxurious. Built of green-painted corrugated iron (hence the name 'Tin Town' or 'Tin City') and lined inside with wood, they were fitted with coal-burning grates to withstand the rigours of a Peak District winter at over 800 feet (243m) above the sea.

The Tin Town community was a lively and vigorous one. Social life revolved around the recreation hall, which was equipped with two billiard tables and a well-stocked library. Functions held there included regular dances, whist drives, film shows and concerts by village children. The recreation ground was known as the Abbey Field, and was the scene of a grand parade and sports day to mark the coronation of King Edward VII in 1902. It was here also that Birchinlee's two football teams and cricket team played their home games against opponents from the neighbouring Hope Valley villages.

At its peak during the fifteen short years that Tin Town existed, nearly 1000 people lived there, and all recollections of it seem to be of a happy, well-regulated community. But it was always destined to be a temporary home for the families whose fathers were working on the dams. The upper dam, Howden, was the first to be completed in 1912, and the lower, Derwent Dam followed three years afterwards.

Looking north along the top road in Birchinlee village. Right is 'Harry the Jew's' tailors and outfitters shop. (By courtesy of Prof. Brian Robinson)

72

The wedding feast of Harry Ashworth and Vinetta Dobson on Boxing Day, 1910. This rare photograph shows the beautifully-furnished interiors of the workmen's 'huts'. Note the canary in its cage above the table. (By courtesy of Prof. Brian Robinson)

As the nomadic navvies and their families started to drift away from Birchinlee to the next project in December, 1913, the demolition of the huts began and by the following August, about half of them had disappeared, some to be reused locally as barns or meeting halls.

Two more ancient villages were lost with the construction of the Ladybower Dam, the third in the series of Derwent Dams, between 1935-43. This earth-core construction dam resulted in the demolition and flooding of the sites of the villages of Derwent, on the eastern side of the valley, and Ashopton, an ancient coaching stop on the Snake Road (now the A57). Most of the villagers were rehoused in purpose-built accommodation at Yorkshire Bridge, under the massive earthwork embankment of the Ladybower Dam.

Among the buildings lost at Derwent was the stately Jacobean pile of Derwent Hall, which dated from 1672 and used as a shooting lodge by the Dukes of Norfolk. It later became one of the first youth hostels in the Peak. In times of extreme drought, the foundations of the hall, the packhorse bridge and the parish church of St John and James are revealed in the exposed silt.

There is very little to be seen on the site of Birchinlee today, in the trees by the roadside on the western side of the lower part of the Derwent Reservoir. The most conspicuous remains are the red brick foundations of the incinerator, where the village rubbish was burned. The rectangular foundations of some of the buildings, and the terraces on which they were built, can still just be made out among the trees, but these are on private land, and very little else remains.

But one name still acts as a memorial to this short-lived community. The sharp bend in the road as it rounds Ouzelden Clough and enters the village site is still known as Sutton's Corner, and commemorates the much-loved navvy missioner, George Eustace Sutton, who played such a significant part in the lives of the navvies and their families. With his family of six children, he was the last to leave the site of Birchinlee village in 1915, but he left behind an account of what life was like there in *The Story of Birchinlee – A Memento of Twelve Years in the Workmen's Village* which was published in 1914, from which this excerpt is taken from the conclusion:

> *We trust that when Birchinlee is levelled to the ground, many may look back with pleasure and gratitude to the first decade of the twentieth century, and pressing ahead in all that is pure and noble, may build up characters that shall be more stable, even, than those huge masonry walls built by them in the Derwent Valley, and more lasting than the non-abiding 'city of Tin Town'.*

'For here we have no continuing city, but we seek one to come.'
Hebrews xiii.14

☙❦

RULES OF THE DOSS HOUSE

Among the strict rules and regulations laid down by the Derwent Valley Water Board for navvies in temporary accommodation in the 'Doss House' at Hollinclough, near Birchinlee, were the following:

No Applicant will be admitted unless he consents to have his clothes disinfected and to take a bath.

The price charged is 6d (2½p) each per night, which must be paid on entering. In exchange the Applicant will receive a numbered ticket, entitling him to a night's lodging with the use of clean night-shirt, bed, bed-clothes and use of common fire.

Provisions can be obtained from the care-taker at the following prices:

Mug of tea, with milk and sugar	1d (approx ⅖p)
Potatoes (per meal)	1d
Bacon (per lb)	8d (3p)
Bread (per lb)	1d
Porridge (with pt of milk)	1d
Soup	1d

No one is permitted to bring intoxicating drink of any kind whatever into the House, and anyone infringing this rule will be at once turned out, and, if in employment on the Works, will be paid off and will have no further chance of being engaged.

CHAPTER NINE

Something in the Air

I'd been asked by BBC TV to do a piece to camera at one of the 50 or so aircraft wrecks which litter the Dark Peak moors, and which have claimed the lives of about 200 pilots and crew since the Second World War.

Knowing TV's requirement for a dramatic story and a not-too-long walk for the camera crew, the site I'd chosen to take them to was one of the most famous, and accessible. I chose the B-29 Superfortress on Higher Shelf Stones, the south-westernmost buttress of 2076ft/633m Bleaklow, such a prominent landmark to motorists as they drop down into Glossop after crossing the notorious Snake Pass.

The story of the giant, four-engined Superfortress 44-61999 'Over Exposed' was an interesting one. It had played an important role in the initial atomic bomb tests over Bikini Atoll in the South Pacific in 1946. Code named Operation Crossbow, this project saw the explosion of two nuclear bombs, one over the atoll and one underwater.

Eight B-29s were specially modified to carry 25 cameras in order that they could undertake a photo reconnaissance role. Over Exposed was one of these, and its task was to photograph the bombing aircraft as the nuclear bomb left the bomb bay. Other photo-reconnaissance Superfortresses circled the massive explosion, recording the infamous mushroom cloud.

On July 1, 1946, as part of Operation Able Day, Over Exposed accompanied the B-29 Dave's Dream which dropped the deadly device over the atoll aiming it at the target ship, Nevada. Immediately the cameras installed in Over Exposed started rolling, and the aircraft dived 1000 feet to be a relatively safe 7 miles away when the bomb actually detonated. Three weeks later, it also filmed the results of the second, underwater explosion. So Over Exposed already had a place in military history.

Two years later, the closure of the road links into Berlin by the occupying forces of the Soviet Union, caused the Berlin Airlift, and Over Exposed was again used on photo reconnaissance missions over Russian-occupied Germany during the Berlin Airlift. As transport aircraft flew in food, fuel and other supplies into Berlin, B-29s like Over Exposed mingled with them to spy on and map the Soviet territory passed over en route.

By 3 November, 1948, Over Exposed was part of the 16th Photographic Reconnaissance Squadron, Strategic Air Command, stationed at the famous former Dambusters' base at RAF Scampton in Lincolnshire. It was from this airfield that Guy Gibson and his brave crews of 617 Squadron had taken off in their Lancasters to attack the Ruhr Valley dams five years before.

Over Exposed's young crew, led by the fresh-faced thirty-three-year-old Captain Langdon P. Tanner, must have been in a happy, demob mood because they had all just completed their service overseas, and were due to return home to the USA in just three days' time.

A routine flight had been scheduled for them to take the payroll to the USAF staff at RAF Burtonwood, near Warrington, which served as a service depot for the Berlin Airlift, plus some sacks of mail for the folks back home in the United States. It was a mere 25-minute flight, and when Tanner was briefed by Flight Control he was told that he could expect broken clouds at 2000 to 4000 feet, with visibility of between 4 and 6 miles.

What happened next, in those days before the advent of 'black box' flight recorders, no one can ever be sure. But maybe Captain Tanner encountered those 'broken clouds' over Bleaklow, and maybe he nosed down through them to fix his position. Whatever actually happened, twenty minutes into the flight, Over Exposed crashed into the peat hags and groughs just to the north of the 2000-foot/600m summit of Higher Shelf Stones. All 13 crew members were killed either outright or in the flames as the aircraft caught fire.

When Over Exposed failed to arrive at Burtonwood, an air search was immediately instigated, and the blazing wreckage of the downed aircraft was spotted by the afternoon. By coincidence, members of the RAF Mountain Rescue Unit based at Harpur Hill, near Buxton, were on an exercise just 2½ miles away from the crash site. They picked up the chilling message that a 'Superfort' was down in flames on Higher Shelf Stones, and they set off immediately to render what assistance they could.

By this time, the weather had typically deteriorated to low mist and drizzling rain, but as two members of the team approached from the Snake Summit, they saw the Superfortress's gigantic tail fin looming in front of them, with a fire blazing uncontrolled over the rest of the fuselage. As they stumbled across the groughs to get to the wreckage, the numbing realisation dawned on them that there was nothing they could do to save the crew. They could see several bodies scattered around the burning, twisted wreck of the once-proud aircraft, and a watch found on the wrist of one of the aircrew gave the time of the crash as 10.50am.

By now, night was closing in, and as firemen from Glossop arrived on the

77

scene to put out the blaze, other members of the team arrived and conducted a search of the quarter of a mile over which the wreckage was spread, and eight bodies were found.

Next morning, about 50 searchers completed the sad task of finding and recovering the remaining five bodies. Again, these were the days before such things as helicopter rescues, and they had to be individually stretchered across the 3 miles of rough moorland to reach the Snake road.

There is still a surprising amount of the Superfortress left at the crash site, including the remains of the four Wright Cyclone engines and bits of perspex, twisted steel and aluminium. So when I took the producer of the programme on a 'recce' to show her where it was, she was suitably impressed. Local people from Glossop have erected a simple plaque telling the tragic story of Over Exposed, and there are usually poppy wreaths and small wooden crosses around, in remembrance of the 13 young aircrew who lost their lives. There's no doubt that it is still a spooky spot.

Nevertheless, after a very brief look round and a short walk to the summit, I was surprised when Trudy the producer said she had seen enough and wanted to get back to her car. 'I just feel a bit uncomfortable here,' she said, mentioning that the ability of 'second sight' ran in her family. Of course, I'd told Trudy of the ghost story which is attached to the wreck of Over Exposed, which was one of the reasons we were there, and it may have just been an association of ideas. The actual filming took place some weeks later without incident, but most people seem to feel something a little spine-chilling in the air around the sad wreck of Over Exposed.

The ghostly story is that some time in the early 1970s, an aviation historian from Glossop had been at the wreck site during a heavy rain storm, and he uncovered what he thought was a brass washer. When he cleaned the clinging black peat from it, he was astonished to find it was a gold wedding ring, inscribed with the name of the captain of the doomed aircraft – Langdon P. Tanner.

Soon after his chilling discovery, he took a party of aircraft enthusiasts to the site to show them where he had made the find. 'I bent down to show them where I found the ring and when I looked up, they had scarpered and were 10 to 15 yards away,' he recalled later. 'When I caught up with them they were ashen-faced. They said they had seen someone standing behind me, looking down and dressed in full flying uniform.'

They told the man, who had neither seen nor felt anything himself, that they had seen enough thank you, and they set off for the road and he has never heard from them again.

Stories of phantom aircraft, air crashes and ghostly airmen are not uncommon at or around wreck sites on the Dark Peak moors. Among the most common of these are the tales of people seeing low-flying Avro Lancaster bombers over the Derwent moors, or the Ladybower, Derwent or Howden Reservoirs in the Upper Derwent Valley.

The public fascination with these slightly macabre remains seems to be unabated. There are at least two best-selling books on aircraft wrecks in the Peak District, and when in a previous existence I ran the programme of guided walks for the Peak District National Park Authority, the ones always guaranteed to be overbooked and with waiting lists were those to moorland aircraft wreck sites.

As already mentioned, the Derwent Valley was one of several sites throughout Britain which were used by Wing Commander Guy Gibson's legendary 617 Squadron – the Dambusters – during their brief period of training before their epic raid on the Ruhr dams in 1943. In fact, very few flights were made over the Derwent Dams and certainly none of Barnes Wallis's famous 'bouncing bombs' were ever dropped there.

The valley's superficial resemblance to the steep, wooded valleys of the Ruhr, and the twin towers on the Derwent and Howden Dams (the Ladybower Dam was then still under construction) to the German Moehne and Eder Dams, made it the perfect location to practise the necessary low-level flying skills required.

Following a series of very popular reunions and flypasts on the site in the 1980s, all new pilots of the present 617 Squadron apparently make their 'maiden flights' in their Tornado jets over the valley. The Derwent Valley was also the scene for the still-popular and often-repeated 1955 film of *The Dambusters*, starring Michael Redgrave as Barnes Wallis and Richard Todd as Guy Gibson. Such is the legend of the film and its even more memorable theme march by Eric Coates, Richard Todd was invited to be the guest of honour at the most-recent reunion and flypast by the last surviving flying Lancaster PA 474, City of Lincoln, in 1993.

I was privileged to be invited to fly in PA 474 on the occasion of Air Vice Marshal Arthur 'Bomber' Harris's ninetieth birthday in 1982, when for four hours I was 'mid-upper gunner' in one of the most exhilarating, but uncomfortable, flights I have ever had. My admiration for those brave Second World War aircrews is complete.

Although none of the Lancasters was lost in these training flights (unlike on the actual raid, when eight out of 19 aircraft did not return and 53 aircrew out of 133 lost their lives), ghostly figures of flaming airmen have

The East Tower of the Derwent Dam.

The memorial to the members of 617 Squadron in the West Tower, Derwent Dam.

Avro Lancaster PA 474 flying over the Derwent Reservoir in 1988. (Photo: David Broadbent, courtesy Peter Pedley Postcards)

been reported around the Derwent Dam, and low-flying Lancasters have consistently been reported sighted over the moors around.

Then there is the story of the typically opportunistic farmer who collected some possibly usable pieces of wreckage from a downed Bristol Blenheim bomber on Sykes Moor near Glossop. He took them back to his farm and stored them in a barn.

But one day soon afterwards, he and his son were astonished to see the barn 'almost shake itself to pieces'. They immediately took the wreckage back to the crash site, and the hauntings stopped.

A similar fate happened to a friend who had been given a propeller from the aircraft. Within months of him taking it home, a series of misfortunes befell him, including bankruptcy and desertion by his wife and children.

Most recently, in March, 1997, the police and emergency services were called out after a number of independent callers had reported a low-flying plane described by eye-witnesses as being 'like an old wartime Lancaster' apparently crashing into the bleak moors at the head of the Howden

82

Reservoir in the middle of the night. Several farmers and gamekeepers saw the aircraft, and reported hearing a huge explosion as the aircraft apparently hit the ground.

A full call-out of the mountain rescue services ensued, with over 100 volunteers, search and rescue dogs and two helicopters searching more than 40 square miles of some of the wildest and most inaccessible moorland in the Peak. The intensive operation was eventually called off after fifteen hours of exhaustive but ultimately fruitless searching. No trace of any kind of crash could be found, and the event remains a complete mystery.

Just as mysterious are the common reports of Unidentified Flying Objects (UFOs) which are regularly and increasingly seen in certain areas of the Peak District hills. The Dark Peak moors again, and the area around the White Peak village of Bonsall – the so-called 'Bonsall Triangle' – seem to be particularly attractive to these weird and unexplained lights in the skies.

Most of them take the form of bright lights seen at night, which in some cases follow cars with a spotlight to the terror of their occupants, while some – silvery metallic in appearance – have even allegedly been seen to land.

Perhaps the most famous unexplained illuminations are the Longdendale Lights. Longdendale itself is a bit of a paradox. It crosses some of the highest and wildest moorland in the Peak District, between the 2000-foot summits of Bleaklow and Black Hill, yet the valley floor is crammed with five reservoirs; the constant buzz of the busy A628 Woodhead trunk road between Sheffield and Manchester; strings of ugly electricity pylons, and a former railway line, now used as the Longdendale, or TransPennine, Trail. Wainwright famously described it in his *Pennine Way Companion* as 'Manchester-in-the-country'.

The Longdendale Lights – locally known as 'the Devil's Bonfires' – have been seen haunting the gritstone cloughs on the northern face of Bleaklow for generations. They seem to be concentrated around the hairpin bend known as the Devil's Elbow on the back road from Glossop, to the short, steep-sided valley appropriately known as Shining Clough at the eastern end of the valley, or around the strange isolated mound to the north-west of Bleaklow summit known as Torside Castle.

Torside Castle is a bit of an oddity itself; the green mound in the middle of the heather moorland looks as though it must be man-made, a bit like a Norman motte, and it is recorded in the Derbyshire Sites and Monuments Record (SMR). But paradoxically, the record shows it to be a purely natural, probably glacial, feature.

The Lights take the form of powerful beams and pulsating balls of coloured lights sweeping across the northern gritstone escarpment of Bleaklow and all along the escarpment from Bramah Edge to Shining Clough. They've been seen by local people for many years, but also by the emergency services such as the police and mountain rescue teams, which are often called out to investigate what appears to be a plane crash or accident on the moors.

The source remains an unsolved mystery. Theories include lights from airliners approaching Manchester Airport, ball lightning, marsh gases or 'will o' the wisps', or even electrical discharges from the pylons which stride down the valley. But none of the explanations can account for the range of light phenomena seen in Longdendale. Now there's even a heavily-visited website which is dedicated to the Lights, with a webcam constantly trained, 24 hours a day, on the valley.

Most of these strange lights in the sky can be simply explained, of course, as aircraft lights or meteorological balloons. Others have been described as Unidentified Atmospheric Phenomena (or UAPs), such as the little-understood natural electromagnetic forces which can create glowing energy fields. It has been estimated that around 90 per cent of UFO sightings have down-to-earth explanations.

But that, of course, still leaves an unexplained 10 per cent...

ଔଔ

CHAPTER TEN

Modern Murder Mysteries

Wednesday, 12 January, 1977 was what used to be a typical mid-winter day in the Peak District. The snow had started to fall about mid-morning, and by early afternoon, a veritable blizzard was raging outside my office window in Bakewell.

I was working for the Peak District National Park Authority at the time, but living in Holymoorside, a little mill village on the western outskirts of Chesterfield. That involved a 12-mile trip home across the notorious East Moor, which always caught the first and worst of the snow, in those far off days of real winters.

When the long-awaited announcement went out that those who lived 'over the hill' could leave work and head for home, I must admit that myself and the two colleagues from Chesterfield with whom I shared a car were pretty relieved. We set out immediately into the whiteout, which we knew would be much worse when we ascended to cross the moors.

It was a difficult journey, because the road conditions were terrible and no snow clearance or gritting appeared to have taken place. So as we approached the 1000ft/300m high point at Eastmoor, I and my mate found ourselves out of the car, pushing it up the final gradient before the long descent towards Chesterfield. As we struggled past the few cottages by the side of the road at this desolate spot, we had no idea of the terrible ordeal that an innocent family was undergoing in one of them. The Pottery Cottage case has been described as 'probably the most horrifying chapter in Derbyshire criminal history'.

Thirty-year-old Billy Hughes of Boythorpe, Chesterfield, had been charged with inflicting grievous bodily harm and rape, and was being held on remand at Leicester Gaol. On that fateful day, he was being taken from the prison by taxi to appear before Chesterfield Magistrates Court for committal proceedings to take place. But nearing Chesterfield, he suddenly produced a knife which he had stolen from the prison kitchens and stabbed one of the two prison officers who were accompanying him.

Holding the other officer hostage, he forced the taxi driver to continue through Chesterfield to the lonely escarpment of Stone Edge on the Matlock road, where he forced the warders and the taxi driver to get out. He then made off in the car.

He apparently drove to Beeley Moor, above Chatsworth, where the taxi was later found abandoned having crashed into a drystone wall. Roadblocks were set up, and tracker dogs and Army helicopters were called in to search for the escaped prisoner, who was known to be armed and dangerous. Police officers had actually called at the National Park office in Bakewell for maps of the moors before we had set out for home.

How Hughes, in one of the worst winter blizzards for many years, made his way northwards across the bleak expanses of Beeley and Brampton East Moor to reach the A619 Baslow Road, can only be guessed at. He must have been trying to avoid the road blocks which had been set up. And he must have been very cold and quite desperate by the time he gained entry to Pottery Cottage, the family home of the Morans, by the side of the main road near the summit of Eastmoor.

Richard and Gill Moran lived there with their adopted ten-year-old daughter, Sarah, and Gill's septuagenarian parents, Amy and Arthur Minton. Richard was an executive with a Staveley plastics firm.

When Hughes arrived that snowy day, only the aged Mr and Mrs Minton were in the cottage, living in what today would probably be called the granny flat. He locked Mr Minton, who was seventy-two, and Sarah, when she arrived home from school, in separate rooms and it is believed that he killed them both almost straight away by cutting their throats. He then set about holding the family hostage, isolating individual members as they arrived home, so they could not talk to one another and hatch out an escape plan.

And showing his pure animal cunning, Hughes continued the pretence of taking food every day to the family members he had murdered, to make the others believe they were still alive. He held the family in this frightening grip of terror for more than two days, and police records show that he also committed two sexual assaults during the time of his horrific occupation.

The terrified family were forced to comply with Hughes's demands, and these apparently included two trips out in the Moran's car; once to get some money from Richard Moran's offices, and once, astonishingly, into the centre of Chesterfield for some shopping. Several possible chances of escape apparently occurred until finally seventy-year-old Amy Minton took a fleeting opportunity to tell neighbours of their awful plight. Hughes discovered the attempt, and immediately carried out his final murderous acts by stabbing Richard Moran to death on the landing, and then also knifing Amy Minton as she attempted to make a break to safety.

One of the most extraordinary features of the case was that Derbyshire Police had set up their incident room in the car park of The Highwayman public house at Eastmoor, which is a matter of yards from Pottery Cottage. By the time they finally realised what had been going on almost under their noses at about 8pm on the evening of Friday, 14 January, Hughes had made his escape in one of the Moran's cars, holding the last surviving member of the family, Gill Moran, as hostage.

There followed what can best be described as a Hollywood-style car chase across 20 miles of snow-covered Peak District countryside. A regional crime squad car forced Hughes to pull over as he crossed Tideswell Moor on the A623, but Hughes, holding an axe to Gill Moran's throat, managed to get out and commandeer the police car, and the chase continued.

By this time he was being followed by a veritable convoy of police vehicles, and he must have known his time was up. Eventually, having crossed the desolate Cat and Fiddle Pass and gone into Cheshire, he met another road block across the A357 Macclesfield road near Rainow, and crashed the car into a drystone wall.

A tense, forty-five-minute stand-off ensued, as police negotiators tried to persuade Hughes to release Mrs Moran, who was still being threatened by his axe, while he attempted to take another car. In the meantime, police marksmen had crept into position, using the snow-covered drystone walls as cover.

Finally, Hughes lost his patience and shouted to the officers: 'Your time is up!' and started to attack Gill Moran with the axe. The marksmen immediately opened fire and it was their fourth bullet that killed the crazed axeman.

The inquests on Hughes recorded a verdict of 'justifiable homicide', and 'murder' on his four innocent victims from Pottery Cottage. But the drama was not quite over yet, as on the day of his funeral in his home village of Boythorpe, outraged local people partly filled in Hughes's grave where he was due to be buried. Eventually, he was cremated.

A Home Office inquiry led to criticism of prison staff and the police for not realising what a potentially dangerous psychopath Hughes was. Gill Moran later moved away and remarried, and Pottery Cottage no longer exists, after a name change. But the memories of those unimaginably frightful fifty-five hours for three generations of the Moran family will never be forgotten.

Stephen Downing was well-known in Bakewell in the early 1970s as being a bit of a loner and 'as daft as a brush'. He'd left school at the age of sixteen with the reading age of an eleven-year-old, and since then, he hadn't been able to hold down jobs for long, mainly because of his poor timekeeping.

But most people liked Stephen, and regarded the naïve seventeen-year-old as perfectly harmless. In September, 1973, his latest in a long string of jobs was as a £9.75-a-week gardener at the local cemetery, close to his home on the council estate which overlooks the town to the west.

How Stephen Downing became the centre of one of the most notorious apparent miscarriages of justice in recent criminal history is a tale of local intrigue, secrecy and double-dealing which has attracted the interest of TV and Hollywood movie-makers.

The story of how Stephen Downing had been charged with the murder of thirty-two-year-old secretary Wendy Sewell, how after nine hours of interrogation he had signed a confession, was tried, convicted and served twenty-seven years in prison while constantly protesting his innocence, only to be finally freed after a brave campaign by a local journalist, could not have been dreamed up even by the most skilled dramatist.

Stephen Downing had gone to work, late as usual, on Wednesday, 12 September, 1973, and had come home for lunch and a bottle of pop as he usually did. It was when he went back to work mowing the cemetery that he made the terrible discovery which was to change his life.

To his horror, he found a half-clothed young woman lying face down among the tombstones. She had obviously been the subject of a brutal attack. He knelt down by her side and turned her over to try to offer assistance, at which she raised herself up and shook her head violently, spattering him with blood from her serious head wounds.

Downing immediately went off to get help from the lodge where his boss, the keeper of the cemetery, Wilf Walker, lived. When they returned, Downing was astonished to see that the woman had moved herself and by the time the police and an ambulance arrived, she was still conscious but obviously very badly hurt. A bloodied pickaxe handle lay near the scene, together with discarded items of her clothing.

Wendy Sewell, who worked as a secretary at the local branch of the Forestry Commission, died in hospital from multiple head injuries two days later. Later, the national press were quick to dub her 'the Bakewell tart' in acknowledgement of the allegation that she had a number of men friends and of the town's unique dessert (always, incidentally, known as a pudding in Bakewell; Mr Kipling is responsible for the tarts).

Stephen Downing was immediately taken to Bakewell police station for questioning, where he was interrogated for nine long hours, without cautioning or being offered legal representation. Eventually, feeling tired, cold and hungry, he confessed to the attack on Wendy Sewell. Because of the

Bakewell cemetery – the scene of Wendy Sewell's murder.

accused's poor reading and writing ability, a police officer wrote down his confession which Downing signed, only to later claim that words had been put in his mouth.

Thirteen days later, he retracted the statement, but by that time he had been charged with the murder of Wendy Sewell. At his trial in Derby in February, 1974, Stephen Downing pleaded not guilty, but was unanimously found guilty by the jury, and sentenced to be detained 'at Her Majesty's pleasure' by the judge, with a recommendation that he should serve a sentence of at least seventeen years.

Stephen Downing's distraught parents, Raymond and Juanita, immediately began their campaign for an appeal, but after two attempts had failed, Stephen, who was still protesting his innocence, was deemed in prison parlance 'IDOM' or 'in denial of murder'. Ironically, had he admitted the crime, he would have been allowed home on parole, or released when he had served the seventeen years as recommended by the judge. So by insisting on his innocence of the brutal crime, Downing was further penalised by the system.

Ray and Nita Downing eventually brought the case to the attention of Don Hale, editor of the local weekly newspaper, the *Matlock Mercury*. Don was a keen runner who had been at the *Mercury* for ten undistinguished years, the highlights of which consisted mainly of editing the weekly WI reports and covering the annual well-dressings in the surrounding villages.

Immediately he started investigating the Downing case, Don claims he met a wall of stony silence from both the police and many local people in the Bakewell area. More serious than that were the threatening, anonymous telephone calls, and two cases of attempted hit-and-run 'accidents' which Don was convinced were deliberate.

But what really made Don stick with the case was the overwhelming tide of support and previously unheard 'evidence' from key witnesses (which seemed to have been ignored by the police) which flooded in to his office. Many people in Bakewell, it seemed, knew that Stephen Downing could never have committed the heinous crime of which he was accused – and some even claimed to know who did.

Don Hale, assisted by his loyal staff on the *Mercury*, continued to assiduously collect the evidence and eventually, after a long and often frustrating seven-year campaign, the Downing case was again brought before the appeal court. The judges agreed that the manner in which his confession had been obtained made his conviction 'unsafe'. He was eventually released from prison having served twenty-seven years for a crime he had consistently claimed he did not commit. But his innocence had still not been proved, and Don Hale continued the fight in the European Courts of Justice.

His tenacious fight to free Stephen Downing had taken Don Hale from being a run-of-the-mill local newspaper editor to both Journalist and Man of the Year awards in 2002. He was praised by the Prime Minister and received the Order of the British Empire for his services to campaigning journalism, and today he continues to fight against miscarriages of justice across the world.

Stephen Downing came home to Bakewell amid scenes of great rejoicing, got himself a girlfriend and took a job as a trainee chef in a local restaurant. He was eventually awarded interim compensation from the Home Office to the tune of £250,000. But a detailed Derbyshire police investigation which looked into the circumstances of the case and his conviction in 2003 confirmed that he was still the only suspect in the matter. All other suspects had been ruled out to the satisfaction of the police.

Then in December 2003, Stephen's father, Ray, was jailed for admitting a sex attack on a teenage girl. And the final twist to the tale occurred as this book was being completed when in March, 2004, just as a dramatised version of the case was being shown on television, Stephen Downing was arrested on suspicion of threatening a female witness in his father's case.

So the mysterious and still unsolved case of the 'Murder of the Bakewell Tart' looks as if it will run and run.

ℰℋℐ

Conclusion

We have reached the end of this short excursion into the darker side of Peak District history. It was not the sort of history usually recounted in the tourist guidebooks, but a more uncomfortable trawl through some of the older and blacker aspects of the Peak's ancient, and in some cases more recent, past.

We've seen how, in the isolated valleys of the Dark Peak especially, the old legends, beliefs and religion still seem to flourish, and how they are still being passed down through the generations. We've acknowledged how those two medieval super-heroes – King Arthur and Robin Hood – still loom large in local legend and in the evidence of placenames. And how places like Lud's Church, deep in the Staffordshire Moorlands, cultivate these old beliefs and can still exert a mysterious frisson of danger and excitement.

The vicious murders of Allan and Clara in the Winnats Pass, and the gruesome fate of murderer Anthony Lingard, one of the last people to be publicly gibbeted in England, have been investigated, along with the case of the screaming skull known as Dickie o'Tunstead, whose dogged and restless spirit is alleged to have held up the mighty London and North Eastern Railway.

The story of the epic self-sacrifice of the brave villagers of Eyam in the face of the terrors of bubonic plague during the seventeenth century has been retold in a new light, together with that of the relatively unknown similar but earlier case at nearby Curbar. Then we looked briefly at the history of lead mining in the White Peak, and the rivalries and 'violence on the mine', especially that which took place underground at Magpie Mine, near Sheldon. An excursion down one of the most sinister of these mines – Odin at Castleton – has been recounted, bringing cold shivers back down the spine of the unfortunate author who had to endure the experience all over again.

There are thought to be more than 3000 deserted medieval villages in Britain, and we sought out some of those which are to be found in the green meadows of the Peak. It is interesting to reflect that at one time, some of the loneliest and most deserted places in the Peak District were the sites of thriving villages, and the unbroken pastureland which surrounds them today was once ploughed and sown with arable crops, with people busily at work in the fields where only the ubiquitous sheep graze today.

Birchinlee – or Tin Town – in the Upper Derwent Valley was there for an entirely different reason, as the site of the temporary but surprisingly well-appointed home for the navvies who built the mighty Derwent Dams and their families. Again, nothing remains today to mark the passing of this remarkable and self-contained community.

The Derwent Dams were also the scene of practice runs by the famous 617 'Dambusters' Squadron, before their epic raid on the Ruhr dams in 1943 during the Second World War. But if the stories of some eye witnesses are to be believed, the Dambusters' Lancaster bombers are still to be seen flying over the reservoirs and surrounding moors, and the many aircraft crash sites on the moorland harbour their own mystery and stories of ghostly apparitions. The strange and unexplained story of the Longdendale Lights and UFO sightings all confirm that there's still something in the air over these desolate moorland wastes.

Finally, we looked at a couple of recent murder stories in the Peak, which turned out to be every bit as horrific as those which had gone before.

We started our journey with an account of the ancient Wonders of the Peak, and its description as 'a strange, mountainous, misty, moorish, rocky, wild country.' Tales such as those we have retold in this book seemed to indicate that this seventeenth-century representation of the Peak is still just as applicable today, especially perhaps to visitors coming from the south. But even today's sensation-seeking journalism would not go quite so far as Charles Cotton did in the delightfully-lurid description of the Peak in his version of *The Wonders of the Peake* of 1681:

> *A Country so Deform'd, the Traveller*
> *Would swear those parts Nature's Pudenda were:*
> *Like Warts and Wens, Hills on the one* side swell,*
> *To all but Natives Inaccessible;*
> ***Th'other a blue scrofulous Scum defiles,*
> *Flowing from th'Earths impostumated Boyles;*
> *That seems the steps (Mountains on Mountains thrown)*
> *By which GIANTS stormed the Thunderers Throne,*
> *This from that prospect seems the sulph'rous Flood,*
> *Where sinful Sodom and Gomorrah stood.*

* The Peake
** The Moore-lands

Bibliography

Anon. – *Alderley Edge and its neighbourhood* (1843, reprinted 1972), E.J. Morten

Anon. – *Allan & Clara (n.d.)*, Houghton & Sons

Bell, David – *Derbyshire Tales of Mystery & Murder* (2003), Countryside Books

Bellamy, Rex – *The Peak District Companion* (1981), David & Charles

Clarke, David – *Ghosts and Legends of the Peak District* (1991), Jarrold Publishing

Clarke, David – *Supernatural Peak District* (2000), Robert Hale

Clarke, David with Roberts, Andy – *Twilight of the Celtic Gods* (1996), Cassell

Clifford, John – *Eyam Plague, 1665-66* (2003), published by the author

Collier, Ron & Wilkinson, Roni – *Dark Peak Aircraft Wrecks 1* (1997), Leo Cooper

Daniel, Clarence – *Ghosts of Derbyshire* (1973), Dalesman Publishing

Daniel, Clarence – *Derbyshire Traditions* (1975), Dalesman Publishing

Daniel, Clarence – *The Story of the Eyam Plague* (1977), published by the author

Dobson, R.B. and Taylor, J – *Rymes of Robin Hood, an Introduction to the English Outlaw* (1997), Sutton Publishing

Doyle, Sir Arthur Conan – *The Terror of Blue John Gap* (1990 edition), Blitz Editions

Ford, Trevor D. & Rieuwerts, J.H. – *Lead Mining in the Peak District* (1968), Peak Park Joint Planning Board

Hale, Don with Huns, Marika & McGregor, Hamish – *Town without Pity* (2002), Century

Holt, J.C. – *Robin Hood* (1989), Thames & Hudson

McMeeken, Louis – *Peak Place-names* (2003), Halsgrove Publishing

Naylor, Peter J. – *Celtic Derbyshire* (1983), J.H. Hall

Pickford, Doug – *Magic, Myth & Memories in and around the Peak District* (1993), Sigma Leisure

Rhodes, John – *Derbyshire Lead Mining in the Eighteenth Century* (1973), University of Sheffield Institute of Education

Rieuwerts, J.H. – *Glossary of Derbyshire Lead Mining Terms* (1998), Peak District Mines Historical Society

Robinson, Brian – *Memories of Tintown* (2002), J.W. Northend

Robinson, Brian ed. – *The Seven Blunders of the Peak* (1994), Scarthin Books

Sharpe, Neville T. – *Peakland Pickings* (1999), Churnet Valley Books

trans. Stone, Brian – *Sir Gawain and the Green Knight* (1959), Penguin

Smith, Claire E. – *The Causes and Effects of the Violence at Magpie Mine* (1989), unpub.

Smith, Iain J. – *The Dambusters Raid – Military or Morale Value?* (1999), unpub.

Smith, Roland – *First and Last* (1978), Peak Park Joint Planning Board

Smith, Roly ed. – *Kinder Scout – Portrait of a Mountain* (2002), Derbyshire County Council